I0198376

Games of Skill:
CHESS, DRAUGHTS;
DOMINOES; BILLIARDS;
BAGATELLE;
BACKGAMMON;
ETC.

CHESS

Here, on a pigmy field, two armies spread!
This, pale as new fall'n snow—that, blushing red
Intense the interest that their leaders take,
As though a kingdom were indeed at stake.

OF all sedentary games, Chess is undoubtedly the most eminent. It is played in every civilized nation in the world, from Siberia to Rome—from Iceland to the wilds of Africa; and has been the delight of emperors, kings, warriors, philosophers, and mankind in general, for ages past. Various accounts have been given of its origin, but although it can be traced back to the most remote antiquity, we have no satisfactory proofs of the place where, or the person by whom it was invented; but whoever he was, it is certain that he must have been a man of profound thought. Some say, it was first played at the siege of Troy, having been invented by Palamedes to amuse the Grecian chiefs, disgusted with the tediousness of the siege; but the most probable conjecture is that of Bochartus, who makes it of oriental extraction, and to come to us from Persia, through Arabia; as most of the terms employed in the game are either corruptions or translations from Persic or Arabic words. Thus, check is plainly derived from the Persian *schach*, or king; and *mat*, in the same language, signifies dead; hence, *checkmate*, or the king is dead. In Hindostan and China the game has been practised from time immemorial.

Chess is a capital mental exercise; nothing in it is governed by chance; judgment is everything; a player, therefore, cannot lay the blame of his losing on fortune but must ascribe his miscarriages to deficiency of judgment, or inattention. It acts strongly, too, on the sense of honour; irascible persons should, therefore, avoid it, unless they have learned to acknowledge that the acutest minds may be guilty of an oversight. It has one splendid advantage over almost all other sedentary games—that its lovers do not play at it for wagers, the honour of the victory being the conqueror's only reward. It may be called a representation of war in miniature; two little armies of different colours are drawn up opposite each other in the order of battle, prepared for mutual attack, and to take prisoner the king of the opposite party.

THE BOARD AND THE POSITION OF THE MEN.

The game of Chess is played by two persons on a board of sixty-four squares, alternately black (or any other dark colour) and white, with sixteen pieces on either side, which are also coloured black (or red) and white to distinguish those belonging to each player. The pieces consist of a King, a Queen, two Rooks (or Castles), two Bishops, two Knights, and eight Pawns. Each player has a perfect set, which are arranged on the board in the order shown in the following diagram.

THE PIECES ARRAYED IN ORDER OF BATTLE.

The pieces have their separate moves, and the object of the game is to place your adversary's king in such a position as to render him *hors de combat*; the player who first succeeds in accomplishing that end wins. All the pieces *take* in the direction of their moves, except the pawn; and when they take, they do not, as in Draughts, move into the square beyond, but into that occupied by the piece attacked. The captured piece is then removed from the board, and is out of the game altogether. In placing the board between the players, a white square is always to the right hand of each player. At the commencement of the game the position of the pieces (taking the white side as an example) is as follows:—The king's rook is on the white corner square; next comes the king's knight, next to that the king's bishop, then the king, and next to him the queen, who stands always on her own colour—black queen on a black square, white queen on a white square. This is considered the key-note of the whole arrangement, most young players commencing to place the men by putting the queen on her own square. Next to the queen stands the queen's bishop, next to that the queen's knight, and on the black corner square the queen's rook. The pawns stand in the second row of squares, immediately in front of the pieces, as shown in the diagram. The pieces and pawns on black's side are placed in exactly corresponding positions, on the opposite side of the board, the colours of the squares being of course reversed—the queen standing on a black square, and so on. In play it is usual to call the king, queen, rooks, bishops, and knights *pieces*, and the pawns *men*.

Bishop.   Rook or Castle.   King.   Queen.   Knight.   Pawn.

THE MOVES AND POWERS OF THE VARIOUS PIECES.

THE KING.—The king is the most important piece; the sole object of the game being to hem him in, so that he cannot move without going into such a situation as would render him liable to be taken if he were not a king. He is then *checkmated*, and must surrender. He steps only from one square to the next at a time, but in any direction whatever, either forward, backward, sideways, or diagonally; he can also take any of the enemy's men in any square adjoining to him, so that he does not place himself in *check*; that is, in such a situation that, were he not a king, he could be taken by the enemy. The king is never actually taken; but if he be in check, and can neither take the attacking piece, interpose one of his own, nor move without being in check from another of his opponent's pieces, he loses the game. Whenever the king is attacked, the adverse player must cry " check," which is a warning to the monarch either to defend himself, or to move into a place of safety. The two kings can never stand on adjacent squares, since they would mutually place each other in check.

THE QUEEN is the most powerful piece on the board; she moves, like the king, in any direction—as far as she pleases, provided the squares in her line of march be unoccupied—upwards, downwards, sideways, or diagonally, combining the moves of all the pieces except that of the knight; and herein consists her superiority and value over any other piece, even if it be aided by a pawn.

THE ROOKS (or CASTLES) are next in importance to the queen. Their progress is backward, forward, or sideways, but not diagonally; and they may move as far as the field is open.

THE BISHOP moves diagonally only, as far as the squares are open. The bishop, therefore, always keeps the same coloured square as that on which he is placed at the beginning of the game.

THE KNIGHT is particularly useful at the beginning of the game, and should be one of the first pieces brought into play. The knight moves in a peculiar way, the move being one square forward, backward, or sideways, and then to another square (of a different colour to, and further removed from, that on which he originally stood) diagonally. Or you may reverse the order of the explanation by saying one square diagonally and then to another square (of a different colour to, and further removed from that on which he originally stood) in a lateral or vertical direction. The move is, in fact, a combination, though limited in distance, of the moves of the castle and the bishop. Remember that the knight must always be played two squares from his starting-point, and to a different coloured square. Thus, at the beginning of the game, the white king's knight moves to a white square, and the white queen's knight to a black square. A knight may be placed on any one square of the board, and moved hence into every one of the other squares in sixty-three moves. We give an example of this curious problem at the end of the article.

THE PAWNS.—A pawn, at his *first* move, may advance either one or two squares straight forward; but after having once moved, he can only advance a single square at a time. In capturing an adverse piece, however, a pawn moves one square diagonally either right or left: but the pawn never moves backward. The pawn is the only man whose mode of taking differs from his ordinary move. On arriving at an eighth square, or the extreme line of the board, a pawn assumes the power of *any piece his owner chooses to call for;* so that a player may have two or more queens, three or more rooks, bishops, or knights, on the board at one time. This is called *queening* a pawn (as the original rule probably was that a pawn so advanced was exchanged for a queen only). If, on moving two squares, a pawn is placed by the side of an adverse pawn which has arrived at the fifth square, the advanced adverse pawn may take the other *in passing* in exactly the same manner as if the latter had moved but one square. This is called taking *en passant*, a power confined to the pawns.

TECHNICAL TERMS USED IN THE GAME.

ATTACK.—When one of your pieces is so situated that, were it your turn to move, you could capture an adverse man, you are said to *attack* such man.

CASTLING is a compound move of king and castle, in which the castle is brought to the square next the king, and the latter moved to the other side of the castle. This is the only opportunity during the game that the king has of moving two squares at one step. Various conditions attached to this combined move of king and castle are explained in Law XIV.

CHECK.—When the king is within the range of an adverse piece or pawn, he is said to be *in check*; he must then either move to a square where he will be out of check, interpose a piece or pawn between himself and the attacking piece, or take the latter, either himself or by one of his pieces.

CHECK BY DISCOVERY is given when, by moving a piece or pawn, check is suddenly *discovered* or *unfolded* from another piece, whose attack was previously masked by the piece now moved.

CHECKMATE.—The king being in check, must get out of check by one or other of the means already stated; if he cannot either take the attacking piece, interpose, or move to a square not commanded by his adversary's forces, he is *checkmated*, and loses the game.

COUNTER ATTACK.—When you repel an attack by playing yourself an attacking, instead of a defensive move, you make a *counter attack*, which is often the strongest kind of defence. Suppose your adversary to assail a knight, and you leave the knight *en prise*, and *counter attack* his queen, this defends your knight for the moment; as, were he to take it, you would capture his queen.

DOUBLE CHECK is given when, by moving a piece, check is not only given by the piece actually moved, but also *discovered* from another piece by the removal of the first.

DOUBLED PAWN.—The leading pawn when two are on the same file, the leader having reached that file by taking an adverse piece or pawn.

DRAWN GAME.—When neither player can checkmate, the game is *drawn*. Such an ending is in many cases inevitable; as when both sides are reduced to king against king without pawns; kings supported only by two knights, or a knight and bishop, with which pieces only, mate is impossible; when one player insists on giving a series of checks and the other refuses to make any other move than from square to square and back again, which constitutes *perpetual check*. Stalemate, also (see p. 559), is reckoned a drawn game. It is considered a drawn game when both players remain with almost or quite an equality of force, as with queen against queen, rook against rook, knight against rook, bishop against rook, etc., except in particular situations when the attacking force can obtain some decided advantage. A game is also drawn when the player left with an inferior force, as bishop against queen, rook against queen, king against two bishops, gives notice that he will count, and his opponent fails to mate within *fifty* moves on either side.

EN PASSANT.—To take a pawn *in passing*. This is a very simple move, though it is not generally understood by young players. When your pawn has advanced to the fifth square, and your opponent, at the first move of his pawn on the next file, pushes it two squares forward, he passes the square guarded by your advanced pawn. You have then the privilege of removing your adversary's pawn and passing into the square which your own guarded, just as if your opponent's pawn had moved one square, instead of two. A pawn only, and not a piece, can be taken *en passant*; and it is at the option of the player whether he take advantage of his privilege or not.

EN PRISE.—This term is used to express the position of a piece or pawn attacked by another and in danger of being taken.

FOOL'S MATE.—It is possible to checkmate in two moves, and this is called *fool's mate*, to mark the ignorance of the party defeated. The following is the form of this mate :—

WHITE.	BLACK.
1 K. Kt. P. two squares	1 K. P. two squares
2 K. B. P. one square	2 Q. mates on her K. R.'s fifth

FORCED MOVE is a move compelled to be made; as, for instance, if you give check, foreseeing that the check can only be met by the interposition on a certain square of a certain piece, such interposition becomes a *forced move*.

FORKING is a term applied to the move of a knight or pawn when it assails two pieces; as when the knight gives check and by the same move attacks a piece; but the word properly refers to the divergent powers of all the pieces.

GAINING A MOVE.—Suppose your adversary to give check with his queen, which queen you drive away by interposing a castle, you here *gain* and he *loses* the move. Philidor says that two lost moves are equal to a pawn. One lost move may cost you the game, and you may frequently win through *gaining a move*.

GAMBIT, a term derived from an Italian word used in wrestling, signifies the offering some apparent advantage to an opponent in order that, should he accept it, he may be the more easily tripped up. In Chess it is used to denote the offering of a pawn or knight with the view, should it be taken, of securing a better position. There are various kinds of gambit in the several openings of the game—as the king's, queen's, Muzio and Allgaier gambits, so called from their inventors, or from the pieces to which the gambit pawn belongs.

GAMBIT PAWN.—The pawn sacrified in opening a gambit, as well as the pawn which captures the offered pawn, are called *gambit pawns*.

INTERPOSE.—To *interpose* is to bring a piece or pawn between your king and the piece that gives him check; or to stop your adversary's attack on a piece by placing between the combatants a piece of your own.

ISOLATED PAWN.—One which stands by itself unsupported by another pawn.

J'ADOUBE.—This term is used when a player touches a piece or pawn in order to *adjust* or place it on its proper square during the game. No player is allowed to touch a piece without moving it, unless he use this word, or its English equivalent.

MAJOR PIECES AND MINOR PIECES.—The queens and rooks are termed major pieces, the bishops and knights minor pieces. The pawns are generally distinguished as "men."

PASSED PAWN.—One which has no adverse pawn in front of it, either on its own file or a file adjoining.

PERPETUAL CHECK is given when a king is in such a position that his opponent insists on attacking him (giving him check at each move) with a piece or pieces so that he cannot escape, although he may have one or more squares in which to take refuge so as to avoid checkmate. The game is then *drawn*.

QUEENING A PAWN is its change into a piece on arriving at the eighth square of a file. The piece selected may be a queen, rook, bishop, or knight; but the pawn *must* be changed directly it moves on to the square. In some situations, the change into a knight is of great importance, as it enables the player to give check by a move not possessed by the queen; but as the powers of the latter combine those of the rook and bishop, it is usual to change the pawn either for queen or knight. It has already been explained that any or all the pawns may be changed into pieces: thus, the player may have two or more queens, three or more rooks, bishops, or knights on the board.

RANK AND FILE.—The horizontal, or lateral, squares are termed *ranks*; the perpendicular, or vertical, squares are termed *files*.

Scholar's Mate, a checkmate which can be given in four moves, as described on page 562.

Smothered Mate is a term used to express the position of a king so surrounded by his own pieces that he is obliged to surrender to the attack of a pawn or knight.

Stalemate is such a position of your king (not being in check, and not having any other piece which he can move) that he can move to no square without going into check. . In stalemate the game is *drawn*.

Supporting a Piece is guarding one piece with another.

Winning the Exchange is obtaining a major for a minor piece, or one of the latter for a pawn.

LAWS OF CHESS.

· I. The board is to be placed with a white square to the right hand of each player.

II. If any error have been committed in the placing of the board or men, the game must be recommenced; but either player may claim that the game shall be finished as it stands if four moves have been completed on each side. ·

III. The players draw for the move in the first game, after which the move is to be taken alternately in the succeeding games of the same sitting.

IV. The player who gives odds is entitled to the first move.

V. A move once made, by your having moved a piece and left hold of it, cannot be retracted.

VI. If you touch a piece, you must play that piece; but as long as you retain your hold, you can play it to any legitimate square. If you touch a piece or pawn that cannot move, your opponent may compel you to play your king, unless the king be unable to move. When you touch a piece for the mere purpose of adjusting it, you are bound to say so, using the French term " j'adoube," or its English equivalent.

VII. If you make a false move, your opponent may, at his pleasure, either cause you to retract it and move your king, or claim that the false move shall stand, or that you shall make a legal move with the same piece.

VIII. If you touch one of your opponent's men, he may compel you to take that man; or if that be impossible, to move your king, provided it can be moved without going into check.

IX. If, on the king being checked, due notice is not given by the word " check," the player whose king is attacked is not bound to notice it; but on the check being afterwards detected, all moves subsequently made must, as far as practicable, be recalled.

X. Drawn games count as no games at all in any match, except by agreement among the players.

XI. The time for consideration of a move is not limited; but a player leaving a game unfinished without his opponent's permission, loses such game.

XII. When at the end of a game one player is left with sufficient superiority of force to win—as a king and rook against king, king and two bishops against king, etc.—he who has the greater force must give checkmate within fifty moves on each side, counting from the time notice is given, or the game is drawn.

XIII. Stalemate, and perpetual check if persisted in, constitute drawn games.

XIV. Castling cannot be accomplished under the following circumstances :—If your king has previously moved during the game ; if your king is at the moment in check ; if your king in castling move into check ; if the rook with which your king castles has previously moved ; and if either of the squares crossed by the king is commanded by any piece or pawn of your opponent. Castling is only allowed once in a game. The king can castle either with his own or with the queen's rook.

XV. When a player gives the odds of a rook he may castle on that side of the board from which he has taken the rook, provided the rook's square be empty and he does not otherwise infringe any of the rules for castling, as given in Law XIV.

XVI. If the player touch both king and rook, intending to castle, his adversary may compel him either to move one of the two pieces, or to castle.

XVII. Directly a pawn attains its eighth square it must be exchanged for a queen, rook, bishop, or knight, as the player may choose, but it is not allowed to remain a pawn.

XVIII. No penalty can be enforced for a false move if the other player move a piece subsequent to the false move, and fail to call such false move.

XIX. The saying aloud " check " does not compel the player to give check, unless he have completed the move by quitting the piece in hand ; nor does it compel him to play any piece he has not touched. But if, in consequence of saying "check," the other player moves his king or any other piece, he may retract the move, provided the mistake be detected before a subsequent move be made.

XX. The player who undertakes to win any game or position, and succeeds only in drawing the game, loses it.

XXI. The player who gives odds of a piece may remove it from either side of the king ; but if he gives a pawn only, he must remove the king's bishop's pawn, unless otherwise stipulated.

XXII. The player receiving the odds of a certain number of moves must not move beyond his own half of the board.

XXIII. All cases of dispute are to be referred to a third party, whose decision shall be final.

XXIV. Lookers-on are forbidden to comment upon the game either by way of approval or otherwise.

CHESS NOTATION.

By the simple plan here explained, the player, with board and men before him, can easily follow the moves of a game from written or printed directions. At starting, all the pieces on the board are said to stand on their own squares, and the pawns on the second squares of the pieces. Then, as a pawn or piece moves, each move is distinguished by the name of the square to which it moves, which is that of the piece which originally stood on the first square of the file, together with its number. Each square is reckoned from the side whence the piece started, thus—White queen's second square is black queen's seventh ; or, when the king's pawn moves, he is said to move to his king's third, fourth, fifth, sixth, seventh, or eighth, as the case may be ; and so also of all the other pawns and pieces. This will be better understood by a diagram :—

BLACK.

Q.R.sq. Q.R.8	Q.Kt.sq. Q.Kt.8	Q.B.sq. Q.B.8	Q.sq. Q.8	K.sq. K.8	K.B.sq. K.B.8	K.Kt.sq. K.Kt.8	K.R.sq. K.R.8
Q.R.2 Q.R.7	Q.Kt.2 Q.Kt.7	Q.B.2 Q.B.7	Q.2 Q.7	K.2 K.7	K.B.2 K.B.7	K.Kt.2 K.Kt.7	K.R.2 K.R.7
Q.R.3 Q.R.6	Q.Kt.3 Q.Kt.6	Q.B.3 Q.B.6	Q.3 Q.6	K.3 K.6	K.B.3 K.B.6	K.Kt.3 K.Kt.6	K.R.3 K.R.6
Q.R.4 Q.R.5	Q.Kt.4 Q.Kt.5	Q.B.4 Q.B.5	Q.4 Q.5	K.4 K.5	K.B.4 K.B.5	K.Kt.4 K.Kt.5	K.R.4 K.R.5
Q.R.5 Q.R.4	Q.Kt.5 Q.Kt.4	Q.B.5 Q.B.4	Q.5 Q.4	K.5 K.4	K.B.5 K.B.4	K.Kt.5 K.Kt.4	K.R.5 K.R.4
Q.R.6 Q.R.3	Q.Kt.6 Q.Kt.3	Q.B.6 Q.B.3	Q.6 Q.3	K.6 K.3	K.B.6 K.B.3	K.Kt.6 K.Kt.3	K.R.6 K.R.3
Q.R.7 Q.R.2	Q.Kt.7 Q.Kt.2	Q.B.7 Q.B.2	Q.7 Q.2	K.7 K.2	K.B.7 K.B.2	K.Kt.7 K.Kt.2	K.R.7 K.R.2
Q.R.8 Q.R.sq.	Q.Kt.8 Q.Kt.sq.	Q.B.8 Q.B.sq.	Q.8 Q.sq.	K.8 K.sq.	K.B.8 K.B.sq.	K.Kt.8 K.Kt.sq.	K.R.8 K.R.sq.

WHITE.

It will be seen that each square has two names, one for noting white's moves and the other for black's. In noting a game on paper, this is made plain by placing the moves of each colour in a separate column. Thus, when we write—

WHITE.	BLACK.
1 P. to K. 4	1 P. to K. 4
2 K. Kt. to B. 3	2 Q. Kt. to B. 3,

we mean that white's pawn has moved two squares, that is, to his king's fourth, and that black has replied by also moving his pawn two squares, *i.e.*, to *his* king's fourth; then white moves his king's knight to his king's bishop's third square, and black moves his queen's knight to his queen's bishop's third square. The taking of a piece is thus stated—P. takes P., or B. takes Kt. By this system every move can

36

be clearly stated, as will be seen by the following moves of the little game known as "Scholar's Mate:"—

WHITE.	BLACK.
1 P. to K. 4	1 P. to K. 4.
2 K. B. to Q. B. 4	2 K. B. to Q. B. 4
3 Q. to K. R. 5	3 K. Kt. to K. B. 3
4 Q. takes K. B. P. and mates	

The contractions used in this system of notation are—Ch. for check, sq. for square, K. for king, Q. for queen, R. for rook or castle, B. for bishop, Kt. for knight, and P. for pawn. These letters are used either singly or combined. Thus, when we write K. B. P. to K. R. 8, we mean that the king's bishop's pawn has moved to his own king's rook's eighth square; and so also of the other pieces and pawns. Game I. (p. 570), which is noted completely from first move to last, shows at a glance the entire plan of notation, as given above, which is the one now universally adopted.

ELEMENTARY INSTRUCTIONS, AND ADVICE TO BEGINNERS.

It is usual for each player to begin his game by playing his king's pawn two squares. This, however, is perfectly optional, as the early moves in every game are merely preliminary to the player's grand attack or cautious defence. But they, nevertheless, give to the games their special character of strength or weakness, and in many cases determine the final result. The various openings are known by different names, as already explained under the definition of the term *gambit*. The players move in turn. The object of the game, which is to give the enemy checkmate, can scarcely be effected without some definite plan. The player should therefore look forward through the several moves requisite to bring his men into a given position, and also to provide, from time to time, against his antagonist's attempts to frustrate his design, or to attack him in turn. He must seek to penetrate his adversary's plots from the moves he makes. He is not obliged to take a man when it is in his power; but, when he does, the man with which he takes it must be placed on the square occupied by the man taken.

If the king's pawn be advanced two squares, and the queen's one square, an opening is made both for the queen and the queen's bishop to the king's side of the board; and the king's pawn cannot be taken, without the queen's pawn taking the adversary's man in turn, and supplying his place. If two pawns be advanced side by side, neither defends the other; this is sometimes done to further a plan of attack; the pawn sacrificed on these occasions, and the adverse pawn capturing it, are called *gambit pawns*. After the pawns are advanced two squares, the knights may be brought forward, either to support them or act upon the offensive.

The plan of attack should be gradually formed from the commencement of the game, and each step taken should have a tendency to forward it, unless when it is necessary to thwart the plan of the adversary. The player must not suffer himself to be diverted from a well-concerted project by any collateral advantage; for the taking of a pawn or piece may prove injurious when it leads to a deviation from the principal object. If your plan be discovered and frustrated, it is better to form a new one than to persevere in the old. Look well over the board before you move, that you may notice what piece is attacked, and discover, if possible, what your adversary can do to counteract your moves. A plan may be most effectually concealed by excluding the queens and rooks, or by executing it through the agency of inferior pieces or pawns, or by masking the pieces intended to effect it behind men which have apparently no influence in the game. The skilful player, if his moves be calculated with precision, will sometimes sacrifice his most important pieces without hesitation, in order to mislead his antagonist, or when it is necessary to the accomplishment of his plan; nay, he will often do this intentionally, to lead his opponent into the hope of winning, and checkmate his antagonist when the latter fancies he has the game in his hands. It is common for a good player to conceal his purpose till it is out of his opponent's power to frustrate it, and then to pursue it openly. To give check without having it in your power to follow up your attack, is, in general, bad play. If your checking piece can immediately be repulsed, you lose a move. Never attack, therefore, without good preparation; and if your attack proceed well, do not suffer yourself to be drawn aside by any bait your antagonist may throw in your way. The object in chess is to give checkmate, and not to take pieces. Sacrifice your own when the loss of them will frustrate the line of defence adopted by your opponent.

If your adversary leave a piece unguarded, examine the position to see whether it were left so from necessity, oversight, or design. You do not always gain by taking a piece, for you may be checkmated in consequence of taking even a queen. Be not eager to take an adverse pawn in front of your queen; for, as your antagonist cannot take him, he is frequently a better protection than a man of your own. If you cannot save a piece, endeavour to take one of the enemy's; or, by improving your situation, to obtain a compensation for the loss. When you can take a piece two or more ways, examine which way will be the best. If your antagonist can take the man in return, take it with that man which is of the least value. To exchange man for man, occasionally, is good play, or even to exchange a queen for a rook or knight, when either of these pieces would prevent you from giving mate.

Guard your pieces sufficiently; and if your opponent's position be doubly guarded, let yours be trebly guarded. The more valuable pieces should be guarded by those of inferior worth; for, if your opponent guard his minor piece by another minor piece, and you employ your better piece to take your enemy's, you "lose the exchange." An advanced pawn should be well guarded, for it is often indispensable to a checkmate and may make a queen.

Castling is not always advantageous, as from the confined situation in which it places the king, it sometimes (particularly when the adversary has his knights in play) prevents his escaping out of a subsequent check. It is, however, common to retain the power of castling for some time, and to keep the requisite pawns in their places. For as long as you are able to castle, your opponent will be at a loss on which side to direct his attack; and when he has decided, and brought his main strength to bear on one side, you can frustrate his design by castling on the other. It is not good play to move too soon the three pawns in front of the castled king; but liberty of moving may become necessary to get the king out of check; therefore, it is well at once to move the rook's pawn one square.

Do not crowd your forces too much together, as this restrains their movements; a piece that cannot move is often worse than lost, by standing in the way of others. Endeavour to crowd your antagonist's game, which you may succeed in doing if he bring out his pieces too early, by driving them back with your pawns. Endeavour to open your game by judicious exchanges should you find it getting crowded.

Never make a move without examining whether you be endangered by your opponent's last move, nor without calculating whether it will allow him to harm you by his next. Beware of his knights, as they command different squares at once, and may fork two or more pieces. If a knight command the square of a queen or rook, at the same time that he gives check, the piece must be lost unless the knight can be taken; to avoid this, when a knight is near, move any major pieces to a different colour from that of the square on which your king stands. Do not let an enemy's pawn attack two of your pieces at once. Beware of two, and still more of three pieces, that manifest a design on the same square. Block up the way to such square by one of your pawns or a guarded piece. Your queen should never stand before your king, as, in such a situation, she may be lost, by a guarded rook being brought in her front, in which position you cannot remove your queen, because such a move would leave your king in check, so that you will be obliged to sacrifice her for a rook. When you find your game irretrievably lost, do not prolong it by idle moves, but retire gracefully.

ENDINGS OF GAMES.

The whole purpose of the game being to checkmate your opponent, it is necessary to bring all your forces into such a position as to enable you to attack his king while at the same time you guard your own. Now, in order that you should comprehend the nature both of the attack and the defence, it will be as well that we should explain, somewhat at length, the various methods of check. You are already aware that when the king is within range of an adverse piece or pieces, he is in *check*. And that when (being in check) he cannot escape either by moving to another square, taking the attacking piece, or interposing a piece of his own, he is *checkmated*. This last situation may be formed in several ways: first, by the sole agency of adverse pieces, as if the board were without limits and the attacked king without pieces or pawns; next, by adverse pieces assisted by the sides or limitation of the board; thirdly, by adverse and friendly pieces together; and fourthly, by the joint effect of these separate elements.

As this explanation includes every position of checkmate, it also involves all its consecutive elements; the order of the moves, and the process of producing the situations above referred to, are therefore now before us. As the king, standing on a square away from the side squares, commands eight other squares, the forces sufficient to checkmate him must, in their range, be able to command or control nine squares. Hence no two pieces can force checkmate when the king is on a central square; but three minor pieces can give check to the king in the middle of the board, and force him into the side or corner squares, and there give him mate; but in such case the attacking king must assist.

To render what we have said more easily comprehensible, we annex a diagram showing various methods of forcing checkmate. In the position thus shown we presume the black king to have been forced into the corner square.

BLACK.

WHITE.

Here it will be seen that the black king is not in check, but if he had to be moved he would be stalemated, because he could not move without going into check. White, however, having the move, checkmate can be forced in several ways :—

In *one* move, by the rook checking on the white square beneath the black king; or, by white queen taking black queen.

In *two* moves, by white bishop giving check, which forces black queen to take it, when rook mates as before on white king's rook's seventh square. Or by white queen moving to her fourth square, and giving check, when black queen must take her, and rook mates as before. Or by white queen moving to king's rook's third, when black queen must take her, and rook mates, as before, or bishop mates on king's fifth.

In *three* moves, thus—

1 Q. to Q. 4, ch.	1 Q. takes Q.
2 B. to K. 5, ch.	2 Q. takes B.
3 R. to K. R. 7 mate	

Or thus—

1 B. to K. 5, ch.	1 Q. takes B.
2 Q. to K. R. 3, ch.	2 Q. interposes
3 Q. takes Q., and mates	

Or thus—

1 B. checks	1 Q. takes B.
2 Q. to Q. 4	2 Q. takes Q.
3 R. mates	

In *four* moves, by six different methods, viz. :—

1. B. ch., Q. ch., R. ch., Q. takes Q., and mates.
2. B. ch., Q. ch. at K. R. 3, Q. ch. at Q. B. 3, and R. moves to K. R. 7, and mates.
3. B. ch., Q. ch., K. moves to B.'s 2, and R. mates, or Q. or P. mates.
4. B. ch., Q. ch., R. to K. Kt. 7, and R. or Q. mates.
5. B. ch., Q. ch., R. to Q. 8, and either K. discovers mate by R. moving or Q. or P. mates.
6. B. ch., Q. ch., P. ch., and Q. takes Q., and mates.

In *five* moves—B. ch., Q. ch., P. ch., P. moves and becomes a Q., and either R. or new Q. mates; or, B. ch., Q. ch., P. ch., P. moves and becomes a Kt., discovering check, and R. mates at K. Kt. 7.

Or *perpetual check* may be forced by the bishop giving check. The black queen is obliged to take him, when white queen gives check on K. R. 3rd square. The black queen must interpose; but instead of mating, white queen again gives check on Q. B. 3rd (where B. Q. stands in the diagram), and so on continually.

Lastly, *stalemate* may be given thus—P. moves and gives check, when the black queen must take it; then rook takes Q., and because the king cannot move without going into check with the rook, stalemate is the result.

The study of the foregoing position, and the several methods whereby checkmate from such a position may be accomplished, will familiarize the mind of the young player with the intricacies of the game. These, however, are by no means the only ways of giving mate. For instance, any one superior piece, in conjunction with its own king, can checkmate an isolated king; or any two superior pieces, or inferior pieces assisted by pawns, can give checkmate. We proceed to give a few more examples of endings.

"Simple check" is given by any one piece or pawn; "double check" is given by two pieces attacking at the same time, which occurs when, by giving check with one piece, you at the same time uncover check from another. For instance, look at the position of the pieces in the left-hand diagram below:—

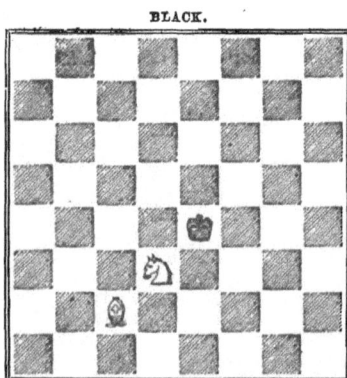

BLACK.

WHITE.
ILLUSTRATION OF DOUBLE CHECK.

BLACK.

WHITE.
ILLUSTRATION OF PERPETUAL CHECK.

The king is not now in check, but if the knight move to his king's bishop's second square, or to his queen's bishop's fifth, he will unmask or discover check from the bishop, and at the same time give check by the knight, thus producing "double check." "Perpetual check" can be given by a single piece, even against a superior force. In the next diagram we see how one queen can always give check; for so soon as either of the black queens interpose, she moves to the other diagonal, and so pins the king that, even with the assistance of two queens, he cannot escape.

As we have already stated, the most simple form of checkmates are those with the queen or rook, when the board is nearly clear towards the end of the game; and every young player should know how to mate in these positions in the smallest number of moves. To checkmate with the queen, unassisted by any piece except her own king, it is necessary to drive the attacked king to a side square, and then to bring up your own king to a square immediately opposite or at not more than a knight's move distant. Then the queen is brought up and speedily gives mate, as seen in the diagram given below.

BLACK.   BLACK.

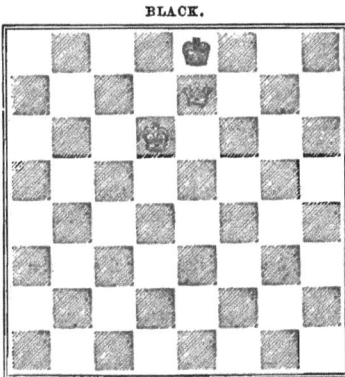 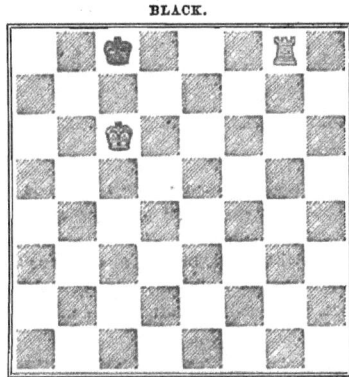

WHITE.   WHITE.

MATE WITH THE QUEEN.   MATE WITH ROOK.

With king and queen against king, checkmate can always be effected, from any part of the board, in at most twenty moves. The way to effect this is first to confine the opposite king to a portion of the board, by placing your queen on a side square of the line in front of the adverse king, and then gradually moving up your king, so that when the two kings are opposite each other you can give check and drive your opponent back to another line. Then proceed as before till you get him in the last row of squares, and getting nearer and nearer with your king, give him mate by moving between the two kings (as in the left-hand diagram), or taking up a position similar to that of the rook in the other diagram.

Mate with the rook is effected in much the same manner as with the queen, the two kings being opposite each other, as in the right-hand diagram above. Here, as the kings may not move next each other, the black king has no escape and is checkmated.

The checkmate with two queens, or with queen and rook, is also very easy. You may effect this without the assistance of the king, in the manner shown in the next diagram. Here the king cannot move out of the rook's check without moving into the line guarded by the queen, and is therefore mated.

BLACK.

WHITE.
MATE WITH QUEEN AND ROOK.

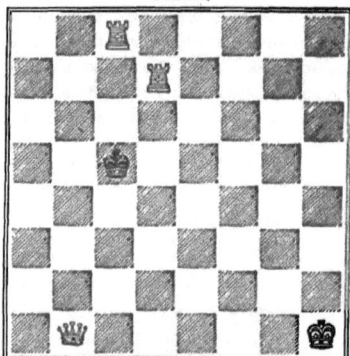

BLACK.

WHITE.
MATE WITH QUEEN AND TWO ROOKS.

Mate with a queen and two rooks is also very easy in any part of the board. All you have to do is to get your pieces into such a position as that shown in the right-hand diagram above.

Mate with rook, bishop, and pawns is a little more difficult. The first of the two following positions shows how rook and bishop may be made to produce a result similar to that arising from the attack of a knight, in addition to the power possessed by a queen.

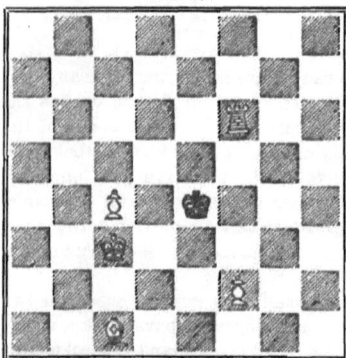

BLACK.

WHITE.
WHITE TO PLAY AND MATE IN TWO MOVES.

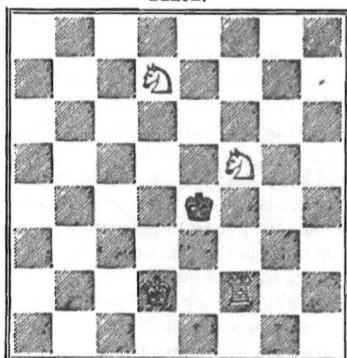

BLACK.

WHITE.
WHITE TO PLAY AND MATE IN TWO MOVES.

Here, although, as will be perceived, the black king is not in check, white undertakes to mate him in two moves. This he effects in the following manner :—First he moves his bishop to queen's knight's second square. The adverse king can then only move to the square diagonal to the rook. The white king moves to the white square to the right (Q. 3rd), discovering check, and mates.

An exceedingly neat and pretty checkmate is shown in the right-hand diagram on the last page. White moves his knight to his king's third square (that between the two kings and the rook). The black king has then but one move, and the rook gives mate on king's bishop's fourth square.

As an illustration of the fourth description of checkmate (see p. 564), take the position shown in the left-hand diagram below. White's king may be anywhere—out of the game, as it were. Here we find the black king encumbered by his own forces :—

BLACK.   BLACK.

WHITE.   WHITE.
WHITE TO PLAY AND MATE IN FOUR MOVES.   WHITE TO PLAY AND MATE IN TWO MOVES.

This is a very ingenious combination, and is introduced in order to explain fully the action of the several pieces. In order to effect the mate, white knight takes the black bishop and gives check. The king can only move into the white square. The other white knight then moves to rook's sixth square and again gives check. The king cannot take the first knight, because he would thus move into check; he must therefore take the second attacking knight with his bishop, when the knight that remains takes the bishop and gives check. The king is obliged to move into one of the black squares, when the white bishop gives check and mates.

In the right-hand diagram above white plays and mates in two moves. First, by giving check with the bishop, when the king is obliged to move into the corner and is mated with the knight. Then, if the pawn be removed and the knight placed on his fifth square, he supports the rook and usually mates in two moves. With the pawn removed and knight at king's bishop's fifth square, white mates in two moves; as he does, also, if the pawn be taken off the board, and knight be placed on king's bishop's fifth and bishop at queen's bishop's fourth; while with the black king in the corner, knight where pawn was, and bishop at king's rook's fifth, the mate is likewise made in two moves. We now proceed to further illustrate our subject by a few

GAMES FOR PRACTICE.

The following games, which we should recommend the beginner to play over several times, are presented, not as the best that could be selected, but as illustrations of certain openings frequently adopted by practised players.

GAME I.—KING'S KNIGHT'S GAMBIT.

WHITE.	BLACK.	WHITE.	BLACK.
1 P. to K. 4	1 P. to K. 4	15 Q. takes Kt., ch.	15 K. to Q.'s sq.
2 P. to K. B. 4	2 P. takes P.	16 B. to Kt. 5, ch.	16 B. to B. 3
3 Kt. to K. B. 3	3 P. to Q. 4	17 Kt. to B. 3	17 B. to Q. 2
4 P. takes P.	4 B. to K. 2	18 R. takes B.	18 K. to B. 2
5 B. to Kt. 5, ch.	5 P. to Q. B. 3	19 B. to B. 4, ch.	19 K. to Kt. 2
6 P. takes P.	6 P. takes P.	20 R. to Q. 6	20 Q. to B. 4
7 B. to B. 4	7 B. to R. 5, ch.	21 Kt. to K. 4	21 Q. takes P.
8 P. to K. Kt. 3	8 P. takes P.	22 R. takes B., ch.	22 Kt. takes R.
9 Castles	9 P. takes P., ch.	23 Q. takes Kt., ch.	23 K. to R. 3
10 K. to R.'s sq.	10 B. to B. 3	24 Kt. to Q. 6	24 K. R. to Q. sq.
11 Kt. to K. 5	11 Kt. to K. R. 3	25 Q. to K. 7, ch.	25 K. to R. 4
12 P. to Q. 4	12 B. takes Kt.	26 B. to Q. 2, ch.	26 Q. takes B.
13 Q. to R. 5	13 Q. takes P.	27 Kt. to B. 4, ch.	27 K. to R. 5
14 B. takes P., ch.	14 Kt. takes B.	28 P. to Kt. 3, mate	

GAME II.—KING'S GAMBIT.

WHITE.	BLACK.	WHITE.	BLACK.
1 P. to K. 4	1 P. to K. 4	22 Q. takes Q.	22 P. takes Q.
2 P. to K. B. 4	2 P. takes P.	23 K.B. takes K.R.P.	23 K. R. to his sq.
3 K. Kt. to B. 3	3 P. to K. Kt. 4	24 B. to Q. B. 2	24 Q. R. to K. 8, ch.
4 P. to K. R. 4	4 P. to K. Kt. 5	25 K. to B. 2	25 K. R. to his 8
5 Kt. to K. 5	5 P. to Q. 3	26 K. B. to B. 5, ch.	26 K. to Q. sq.
6 Kt. takes Kt. P.	6 B. to K. 2	27 K. B. takes Kt. P.	27 Kt. to K. 4
7 P. to Q. 4	7 K.B. takes P., ch.	28 K. B. to his 5	28 Q. R. takes Q. B.
8 Kt. to K. B. 2	8 Q. to K. Kt. 4	29 R. takes R.	29 R. takes R.
9 Q. to K. B. 3	9 Q. to K. Kt. 6	30 Kt. to K. B. 3	30 R. to Q. 8
10 B. to K. 2	10 Kt. to Q. B. 3	31 K. to K. 2	31 R. to Q. 3
11 P. to Q. B. 3	11 K. Kt. to K. B. 3	32 Kt. to Q. 4	32 K. to K. 2
12 K. to B. sq.	12 K. R. to Kt. sq.	33 B. to K. 4	33 K. to B. 3
13 K. Kt. to R. 3	13 Q. B. takes Kt.	34 P. to Q. Kt. 3	34 P. to Q. B. 3
14 R. takes B.	14 Castles	35 P. to Q. R. 3	35 P. to Q. R. 3
15 K. to Kt. sq.	15 Q. R. to K. sq.	36 P. to Q. R. 5	36 P. to Q. B. 4
16 Kt. to Q. 2	16 Q. to K. Kt. 3	37 Kt. to Q. B. 2	37 Kt. to Q. B. 3
17 B. to Q. 3	17 K. Kt. to Kt. 5	38 B. takes Kt.	38 P. takes B.
18 P. to K. 5	18 P. to K. B. 4	39 P. to Q. Kt. 4	39 K. to B. 4
19 R. takes B.	19 P. takes P.	40 Kt. to K. sq.	40 R. to K. Kt. 3
20 R. takes Kt.	20 Q. takes R.	41 K. to B. 2	41 K. to K. 5
21 P. takes P.	21 Q. R. takes P.	42 Kt. to K. B. 3	42 R. to K. Kt. 2

And black eventually wins.

GAME III.—KING'S GAMBIT DECLINED.

WHITE.	BLACK.	WHITE.	BLACK.
1 P. to K. 4	1 P. to K. 4	19 B. to K. 3	19 Q. to K. Kt. 3
2 P. to K. B. 4	2 B. to Q. B. 4	20 Kt. to K. 2	20 P. to K. R. 3
3 Kt. to K. B. 3	3 P. to Q. 3	21 B. to Q. 2	21 P. to Q. 4
4 P. to Q. B. 3	4 Q. B. to K. Kt. 5	22 Kt. to K. B. 4	22 Q. to K. R. 2
5 B. to K. 2	5 Kt. to Q. B. 3	23 P. to K. 5	23 Q. takes Q.
6 P. to Q. Kt. 4	6 B. to Q. Kt. 3	24 Kt. takes Q.	24 Kt. to Q. B. 5
7 P. to Q. Kt. 5	7 Q. Kt. to Q. R. 4	25 B. to Q. Kt. 4	25 K. Kt. to K. 5
8 P. to Q. 4	8 Q. B. takes Kt.	26 B. takes R.	26 R. takes B.
9 B. takes B.	9 P. takes Q. P.	27 Kt. to K. B. 4	27 K. Kt. to Q. 7
10 P. takes P.	10 Q. to K. B. 3	28 B. takes Q. P.	28 K. Kt. takes R.
11 B. to K. 3	11 Kt. to Q. B. 5	29 B. takes Q. Kt.	29 Kt. to Q. 7
12 B. to K. B. 2	12 Q. takes K. B. P.	30 B. to B. Q. 5	30 B. takes Q. P.
13 Castles	13 Kt. to K. B. 3	31 P. to K. 6	31 P. to K. Kt. 4
14 Q. to Q. 3	14 Kt. to Q. R. 4	32 P. to K. 7	32 R. to K. sq.
15 Kt. to Q. B. 3	15 Castles on K. side	33 B. takes K. B. P.	33 P. takes Kt.
16 P. to K. Kt. 3	16 Q. to K. R. 3	34 P. takes P.	34 R. takes K. P.
17 K. to Kt. 2	17 Q. R. to K. sq.	35 R. takes R.	
18 Q. R. to K. sq.	18 K. to R. sq.	And white wins.	

GAME IV.—THE ALLGAIER GAMBIT.

This is a favourite opening with many players, rather showy than safe; but if the second player take the offered knight, he will probably lose the game.

WHITE.	BLACK.	WHITE.	BLACK.
1 P. to K. 4	1 P. to K. 4	11 Q. Kt. to Q. B. 3	11 K. B. to Q. Kt. 5
2 P. to K. B. 4	2 P. takes P.	12 Q. B. to K. B. 4	12 K. Kt. P. takes P.
3 Kt. to K. B. 3	3 P. to K. Kt. 4	13 Q. takes P. [ch.	13 P. to Q. B. 3
4 P. to K. R. 4	4 P. to K. Kt. 5	14 K.R.to K. Kt. sq.,	14 K. to K. R. 2
5 Kt. to K. Kt. 5	5 P. to K. R. 3	15 Q. B. to K. 5	15 K. R. to K. B. sq.
6 Kt. takes K. B. P.	6 K. takes Kt.	16 Q. to K. Kt. 3	16 Q. to K. 2
7 B. to Q. B. 4, ch.	7 P. to Q. 4	17 Q. to K. Kt. 6, ch.	17 K. to K. R. sq.
8 B. takes Q. P., ch.	8 K. to K. Kt. 2	18 Q. takes P., ch.	18 Q. to K. R. 2
9 P. to Q. 4	9 P. to K. B. 6	19 Q.B. takes Kt.,ch.	19 K. R. takes B.
10 K. Kt. P. takes P.	10 K. Kt. to K. B. 3	20 K. R. to K. Kt. 8, mate.	

GAME V.—THE SICILIAN OPENING.

WHITE.	BLACK.	WHITE.	BLACK.
1 P. to K. 4	1 P. to Q. B. 4	11 Castles	11 P. to K. R. 4
2 K. Kt. to B. 3	2 P. to K. 3	12 Kt. to Q. 2	12 P. to K. R. 5
3 P. to Q. 4	3 P. takes P.	13 P. to K. R. 3	13 P. to K. Kt. 4
4 Kt. takes P.	4 K. B. to Q. B. 4	14 P. to Q. R. 3	14 K. R. to K.Kt.,sq.
5 Q. B. to K. 3	5 Q. to Q. Kt. 3	15 P. to Q. Kt. 4	15 Q. to Q. Kt. 3
6 K. Kt. to Q. Kt. 5	6 K. Kt. to B. 3	16 Kt. to Q. B. 4	16 Q. to Q. B. 2
7 Q. B. takes B.	7 Q. takes B.	17 P. to K. B. 3	17 Q. Kt. to K. 4
8 K. Kt. to Q. 6, ch.	8 K. to K. 2	18 Kt. takes Kt.	18 Q. takes Kt.
9 Kt. takes B., ch.	9 K. R. takes Kt.	19 Q. to Q. 2	19 K. R. to K. Kt. 2
10 B. to Q. 3	10 K. Kt. to B. 3	20 Q. R. to Q. sq.	

And white wins.

Game VI.—The Scotch Gambit.

WHITE.	BLACK.	WHITE.	BLACK.
1 P. to K. 4	1 P. to K. 4	22 Q. Kt. to Q. B. 4	22 P. to Q. Kt. 4
2 K. Kt. to B. 3	2 Q. Kt. to B. 3	23 Q. Kt. to R. 5	23 Q. R. to Kt. 3
3 P. to Q. 4	3 K. P. takes P.	24 P. to K. 6	24 B. to K. sq.
4 K. B. to Q. B. 4	4 K. B. to Q. B. 4	25 P. to Q. R. 3	25 K. to Q. 3
5 P. to Q. B. 3	5 K. Kt. to B. 3	26 Q. R. to B. sq.	26 Kt. to K. 2
6 Castles	6 Q. Kt. to R. 4	27 K. R. to Q. sq.	27 K. to Q. B. 2
7 B. P. takes P.	7 Q. Kt. takes K. B.	28 K. Kt. to Q. Kt. 3	28 P. to K. B. 4
8 Q. P. takes K. B.	8 P. to Q. 4	29 K. Kt. to Q. B. 5	29 K. R. to B. 3
9 B. P. tk. P., in pas.	9 Q. takes P.	30 K. Kt. to Q. 7	30 K. R. takes K. P.
10 P. to K. 5	10 Q. takes Q.	31 K. Kt. takes Q. R.	31 R. P. takes K. Kt.
11 K. R. takes Q.	11 K. Kt. to Q. 2	32 Kt. to Kt. 3	32 R. to K. 4
12 P. to Q. Kt. 3	12 Q. Kt. to Kt. 3	33 K. R. to K. sq.	33 R. takes K. R., ch.
13 B. to Q. R. 3	13 K. Kt. to K. B. sq.	34 R. takes R.	34 K. to Q. 3
14 B. takes K. Kt.	14 K. R. takes B.	35 Kt. to Q. 4	35 P. to Q. B. 4
15 Q. Kt. to B. 3	15 P. to Q. B. 3	36 Kt. to Q. B. 2	36 B. to K. B. 2
16 Q. Kt. to K. 4	16 Kt. to Q. 4	37 R. to Q. sq., ch.	37 Kt. to Q. 4
17 Q. Kt. to Q. 6, ch.	17 K. to K. 2	38 Kt. to K. 3	38 P. to Q. B. 5
18 K. Kt. to Q. 4	18 P. to K. Kt. 3	39 Kt. takes Kt.	39 B. takes Kt.
19 K. R. to K. sq.	19 Q. R. to Kt. sq.	40 P. to K. B. 4	40 P. to Q. B. 6
20 Q. R. to Kt. sq.	20 Q. B. to Q. 2	41 K. to Q. B. sq.	41 B. to Q. B. 5
21 P. to Q. Kt. 4.	21 P. to K. B. 3	42 R. takes B. P.	

And white, with a rook against a bishop, and an equal number of pawns, ought to win.

Game VII.—The Centre Gambit.

WHITE.	BLACK.	WHITE.	BLACK.
1 P. to K. 4	1 P. to K. 4	8 Q. B. to K. 3	8 K. Kt. to B. 3
2 K. B. to Q. B. 4	2 K. B. to Q. B. 4	9 Q. P. takes P.	9 Q. Kt. takes P.
3 P. to Q. B. 3	3 Q. to K. 2	10 K. Kt. takes Kt.	10 P. takes Kt.
4 K. Kt. to B. 3	4 Q. Kt. to B. 3	11 B. takes B.	11 P. takes B.
5 P. to Q. 4	5 K. B. to Q. Kt. 3	12 Q. Kt. to Q. 2	12 Castles
6 Castles	6 P. to Q. 3	13 Q. to K. 2,	
7 P. to Q. R. 4	7 P. to Q. R. 4	And ought to win.	

Game VIII.—The Muzio Gambit.

This is a variation of the King's Gambit, in which the first player sacrifices a knight. and unless it is well played is a lost game for the first player.

WHITE.	BLACK.	WHITE.	BLACK.
1 P. to K. 4	1 P. to K. 4	9 Q. Kt. to B. 3	9 K. Kt. to K. 2
2 P. to K. B. 4	2 P. takes P.	10 Q. B. to Q. 2	10 P. to Q. B. 3
3 K. Kt. to B. 3	3 P. to K. Kt. 4	11 Q. R. to Q. sq.	11 Q. to Q. B. 4, ch.
4 K. B. to Q. B. 4	4 P. to K. Kt. 5	12 K. to R. sq.	12 P. to Q. 4
5 Castles	5 P. takes Kt.	13 B. takes Q. P.	13 P. takes B.
6 Q. takes P.	6 Q. to K. B. 3	14 Q. to K. R. 5	14 Q. to Q. 3
7 P. to K. 5	7 Q. takes K. P.	15 Kt. takes P.	15 Q. Kt. to B. 3
8 P. to Q. 3	8 B. to K. R. 3	And white wins.	

Black's fifth move completes the gambit.

MOVING THE KNIGHT OVER ALL THE SQUARES ALTERNATELY.

The problem respecting the placing the knight on any given square, and moving him from that square to every other on the board, has not been thought unworthy the attention of the first mathematicians. Let the knight be placed on any square, and move him from square to square, on the principle of always playing him to that point, from which, in actual play, he would command the fewest other squares; observing, that in reckoning the squares commanded by him you must omit such as he has already covered. If, too, there are two squares, on both of which his powers would be equal, you may move him to either. Try this on the board, with some counters or wafers, placing one on every square; and when you clearly understand it, you may astonish your friends by inviting them to station the knight on any square they like, and engaging to play him, from that square, over the remaining sixty-three in sixty-three moves. When the Automaton Chess-player was last exhibited in England, this was made part of the wonders he accomplished, though as the above plan was not then known here, he could not adopt it, but used something like the method laid down by Euler, a diagram illustrative of which we subjoin.

As this is a re-entering series of numbers, or interminable route, it does not matter on which square the knight is placed at starting; as, by acquiring the plan by heart, which is soon done, you can play him over all the squares from any given point, his last square being at the distance of a knight's move from his first. It is obvious that this route may be varied many ways.

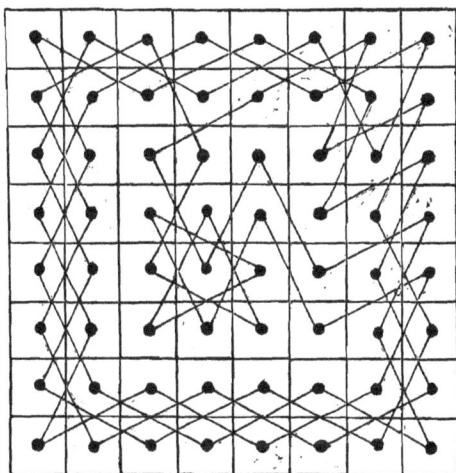

THE AUTOMATON CHESS-PLAYER.

Our subject would hardly be deemed complete without some notice of the celebrated Automaton Chess-player, which at two several periods was exhibited in this country. The machine in question was constructed by M. de Kempelen, a gentleman of Presburg, in Hungary, who came over to England in 1785, and exhibited it for upwards of a twelvemonth, without the mode of operation being discovered. On his death, it was purchased by M. Maelzel, who also came here in 1819, when the invention excited as much wonder as ever. An eye-witness of its performance thus describes it:—

The room where it was exhibited had an inner apartment, within which appeared the figure of a Turk, as large as life, dressed after the Turkish fashion, sitting behind a chest of three feet and a half in length, two feet in breadth, and two feet and a half in height, to which it was attached by the wooden seat on which it sat. The chest was placed upon four castors, which, together with the figure, might be moved to any part of the room.

On the plain surface formed by the top of the chest, in the centre, was raised an immovable chess-board, of handsome dimensions, upon which the figure had its eyes fixed, its right hand and arm being extended on the chest, and its left arm somewhat raised, as if in the attitude of holding a Turkish pipe, which was originally placed in its right hand.

The exhibitor proceeded by wheeling the chest to the entrance of the apartment within which it stood, in front of the spectators. He then opened certain doors contrived in the chest, two in the front and two in the back, at the same time pulling out a long shallow drawer made to contain the chess-men, a cushion for the arm of the figure to rest upon, and some counters; two lesser drawers and a green cloth screen, contrived in the body of the figure and its lower parts, were likewise opened, and the Turkish robe which covered them was raised; so that the construction, both of the figure and chest, intentionally was displayed, and the exhibitor introduced a lighted candle into the body of the chest and figure, by which the interior of each was, in a great measure, rendered transparent.

The chest was divided by a partition into two equal chambers; that to the right of the figure was the narrowest, and occupied scarcely one-third of the body of the chest; it was filled with little wheels, levers, cylinders, and other machinery used in clock-work; that to the left contained two wheels, some small barrels with springs, and two quarters of a circle, placed horizontally. The body and lower parts of the figure contained certain tubes, which appeared to be conductors to the machinery. After a sufficient time, during which each spectator satisfied his scruples and curiosity, the exhibitor closed the doors, made some arrangement in the body of the figure, wound up the works with a key inserted into a small opening in the body of the chest, and placed the cushion under the left arm of the figure, which then rested upon it.

In playing a game, the automaton made choice of the white men; it likewise gave the first move. It played with the left hand instead of the right, the right hand being constantly fixed on the chest. This slight incongruity proceeded from inadvertence of the inventor, who did not discover his mistake until the machinery was too far completed to remedy the defect. At the commencement of a game, the automaton made a motion of the head, as if taking a view of the board; the same motion occurred at the close of the game. In making a move it slowly raised its left arm from the cushion placed under it, and directed it toward the square of the piece to be moved. The arm then returned to its natural position on the cushion. Its hand and fingers opened on touching the piece, which it took up and conveyed to any proposed square. The motions were performed with perfect correctness, and the anxiety with which the arm acted, especially in the delicate operation of castling, seemed to be the result of spontaneous feeling; bending at the shoulder, elbow, and knuckles, and cautiously avoiding to touch any other piece than that which had been moved.

On giving check to the king, it moved its head as a signal. When a false move was made by its antagonist, which frequently occurred through curiosity to observe in what manner the automaton would act—as, for instance, if a knight had been moved like a castle—the automaton smote impatiently on the chest with its right hand, replaced the knight in its former square, and would not permit its antagonist to recover his move, but proceeded immediately to move one of its own pieces, thus punishing him for his inattention.

It was considered of importance that the person matched against the automaton should be attentive in moving a piece exactly in the centre of a square; otherwise, the figure, in laying hold of the piece, might sustain some injury in the delicate mechanism of the fingers. If its antagonist hesitated for a considerable time to play, it tapped smartly on the chest with its right hand, as if testifying impatience at the delay.

During the time the automaton was in motion, a low sound of clock-work was heard, as if running down, which ceased soon after the arm was reclined on the cushion. The works were wound up at intervals of ten or twelve moves by the exhibitor, who was usually employed pacing up and down the room; approaching the chest, however, from time to time, on its right side. It was understood that the automaton could not play unless M. De Kempelen, or his substitute, was near to direct its moves; but it is very certain that the whole mystery lay in the chest, and that there could be no connection with the floor, as the inventor advertised his willingness to exhibit at private houses.

And now for the secret of this wonderful deception. Although the automaton beat numerous skilful chess-players, in different countries, its moves were actually directed by a boy concealed within the machinery; so that, in fact, whoever the boy could beat at the game was sure to be conquered by the automaton! This will show that it is in the power of youth to attain such a mastery over chess as to render them capable of competing with capital players of a mature age.

CONCLUDING OBSERVATIONS.

Thus have we dallied and toyed with this royal game, until it has reached a length which its importance alone could warrant. Our duty, rather than our inclination, now urges us to conclude. Fain would we have added a few rich and racy anecdotes of chess-playing, before we closed, but our limits will not allow it. Willingly would we have spoken of that famous king, who made his castle-court a chess-field, on which the pieces played were living squires, some attired in cloth of gold, others in costly vests of ethereal blue, powdered with silver stars; while knights, armed cap-à-pie, gorgeous as for a tournament, pranced over the chequers, at the bidding of the king and his rival in the game, who governed the moves of that splendid field from a canopied balcony above. We should not have forgotten that irascible scion of royalty, in the olden time, who, when beaten by his brother, took up the massive chess-board, and, most unfraternally, broke his victor's head; nor that man, who, by often playing with a hot and testy master, knew his temperament so well, that the instant he gave checkmate he flew like an arrow from the room, to save his sconce from a similar fate to that of the royal player to whom we have just alluded; nor that great individual, who, being under sentence of death, received a peremptory summons to the fatal block when playing a game of chess, and begged that the officer who came to lead him to his doom would bear witness that he had the best of the game. Had we "ample scope and verge enough," we would, with a surpassing pleasure—to ourselves, at least, if not to our readers—relate the mode and manner of our own acquirement of the game. It was under the tall and stately elms of Gray's Inn Gardens where we first learnt to know what check and checkmate meant. Many a night and oft have we, then just emerging from our boyhood, glided forth through a private gateway into that quiet place, and spreading our board upon the grass, played by the light of a full summer moon, until the world, and all that moved upon it, except the kings, the queens, the knights, and those "stout men-at-arms" on the pigmy field beneath us, were forgotten. Our instructor in the game was a fellow-student of legal lore. A "world of waters" is now between us; he became a roamer, and is now, perhaps, while we are thinking of the night when first we beat him, dreaming of that pigmy board beneath the elms of those cool and shady gardens, though reposing, it may be, on a sandy pillow in the wilds of Afric; or, calculating moves on the summit of the Andes; checkmating an Abyssinian chief; or having assumed the turban of the Moslems, squatting in a bower, and playing chess, in outward appearance

A Turk, with an Arab.

DRAUGHTS

"To teach his grandson Draughts, then
His leisure he'd employ,
Until at last the old man
Was beaten by the boy."

DRAUGHTS is a game which it is well to learn prior to commencing Chess. Though by far inferior to that noble pastime, it is at once unobjectionable and amusing. As in the case of Chess, wagers are seldom laid upon Draughts; the game cannot, therefore, be deemed, in any measure, conducive to gambling, which we most earnestly entreat our young readers, on all occasions, to avoid.

The game of Draughts is undoubtedly one of great antiquity; and from the fact that it was found to be familiar to the natives of New Zealand and other uncivilized countries, on their discovery by Europeans, there seems little doubt that in point of age it preceded Chess. It is a favourite game in all civilized countries, in many of which it is known as the ladies' game. In France it is called "Le Jeu des Dames," and in Scotland the draught-board is still popularly known as the "Dam-brod" (the Ladies' board). In 1668 a French mathematician named Mallet, published an elaborate treatise on the game. He was followed in this country by Mr. Payne: and a later writer, Mr. Sturges, has improved upon both. But these books are all too elaborate for beginners, and assume an acquaintance with the main principles of the game which young players do not generally possess.

METHOD OF PLAYING THE GAME.

Draughts is played by two players upon the ordinary chess-board of sixty-four squares, alternately black and white—thirty-two of each. The board is so placed that each player has the two white squares, called the "double corner," at the right-hand side of his own end. Each player has twelve men; each set of twelve being of different colours, usually black and white; the one player taking the black and the other the white. These are placed on the board in the manner shown in the diagram. A full set of draughtmen consists of fifteen of each colour, the extra men being provided to crown those which become kings, and to make the set perfect for backgammon.

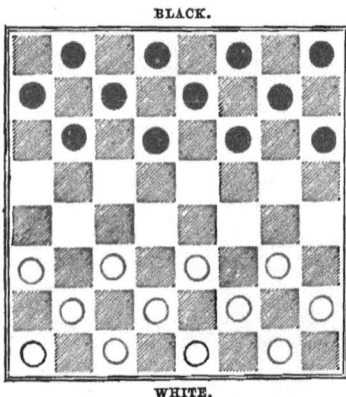

The board is placed between the players, and the pieces are moved diagonally on the white squares, one square at a time. The first player moves a man one square on his side, and then his opponent moves a man in the same manner—always in a diagonal or slanting direction, so that the black squares are never used. A man can only move one square at a time, except when an adverse man stands in the line of his march, with a vacant square beyond, when he leaps over the adverse man to the vacant square; the man so leapt over being thus captured, and removed from the board. The men all "take" in the direction of their moves, and no move can be made unless the square be empty, or a man can be captured by jumping over him to a vacant square. When two or more adverse men are so placed as to have each a vacant square in the diagonal beyond him, and all in the line of march of the man being moved, the player takes as many men as may be so situated, making a second, third, or even fourth leap, as the case may be, in the same move or rather series of moves.

Each player moves alternately; and the object of the game is to capture your opponent's men, or to pin them in their several squares so that they cannot move without being taken. He who first succeeds in clearing the board of his adversary's men, or so pinning them, wins the game.

The men move forwards, on the diagonals only, but when the player succeeds in moving a man to the last row of squares on his opponent's side, such man becomes a King, and is crowned—by the simple process of placing another man of the same colour on the top of him. The kings have the privilege of moving either backwards or forwards on the diagonals. Either player may make as many kings as he can.

NOTATION OF THE GAME.

Below we give a diagram of the board numbered according to the system of notation now universally adopted. A little familiarity with this plan of notation will soon enable you to play the game without seeing the board. Notice that the first two lines of figures downward, from the left upper corner, are all *odd*—5, 13, 21, 29 ; 1, 9, 17, 25; the next two lines are all *even*— 6, 14, 22, 30 ; 2, 10, 18, 26; the next two *odd*—7, 15, 23, 31; 3, 11, 19, 27 ; and the last two *even*—8, 16, 24, 32 ; 4, 12, 20, 28. Therefore, the square immediately beneath or above any other square is eight places distant. Thus, *below* square 11 you have square 19, while *above* it you have square 3, and so on throughout. Observe that the squares from right to left of the player at the upper end of the board, are alternately four and three figures distant :—4, 8, 11, 15, 18, 22, 25, 29 ; while those from left to right are alternately five and four figures distant :—1, 6, 10, 15, 19, 24, 28 ; the same rule holding good if you count from the lower line of figures, 29 to 32, diagonally to the right or left. By this system of notation the player can always bring before his mental vision any position of the men on the board.

BLACK.

[Board diagram numbered 1 through 32]

WHITE.

PRACTICAL EXAMPLES OF THE MODE OF PLAYING.

We will now suppose that two lads sit down to play a game, and that the white men occupy the lower half of the board and have the first move. As only the men on the front rank can move as yet, the player has the choice of moving a man into either of the squares 17, 18, 19, or 20. As the move from 22 to 18 is generally considered a good one to begin with, we will suppose that white makes it. It is black's turn to move a piece ; he, like his adversary, can only advance one of his front rank now ; he may move the man on 9 to 13 or 14, that on 10 to 14 or 15, that on 11 to 15 or 16, and that on 12 to 16 only. The white having moved from 22 to 18, the black then may move, if he please, from 11 to 15. In the next move, the white man on 18 will take the man, so placed by black, on 15, by leaping over his head into 11. It is now black's turn to move, and he, in return, can take white's man which stands in 11, by either of the men standing on 7 or 8. In case he makes the capture with 7, he jumps over the head of the man to be taken into 16; if he prefer taking him with 8, the move will be from 8 to 15. An opportunity here occurs of giving a practical explanation of the *huff*. Supposing, when black had moved from 11 to 15, white had omitted to take him in the manner explained, and made some other move, white would have "stood the huff;" that is, black might have removed from the board the white man that stood on 18, or compelled white to have taken the black man on 15, whichever he pleased. This is "standing the huff;" and be it recollected, that so taking off the man from 18, is not to be considered a move, black having his move after having removed the man, before white can move again. "Huff and move" is the rule. That is, when a player neglects to take a man *en prise*, his opponent removes from the board the man he should have moved, and then moves one of his own men.

The term *en prise* is used to signify a man so placed, with regard to an adverse man, that the latter can take it.

In case the game were in a more advanced state, and that the black man, which at the beginning stood on 4, had been removed, the white man on 18, instead of taking only the black man on 15, would have taken the black man on 8, in addition, by leaping over 15 into 11, and then over 8 into 4, which would be reckoned as one move. In this case, the man in 4, having reached one of the back squares of the enemy (1, 2, 3, and 4), becomes a king, and is crowned.

We will now give a practical example or two of the kingly powers of these "crowned heads." Supposing a black king stood on 29, a white king on 25, a white man on 18, another white king on 19, and a third white king, or a white man, on 27, —if it were black's move, and the board was clear, except only of the pieces that are mentioned, he would take them all thus: from 29 to 22, taking 25; from 22 to 15, taking 18; from 15 to 24, taking 19; and from 24 to 31, taking 27. If, however, the black king only take the first, second, or third of these pieces, he would stand the huff, *i. e.*, the adversary may either remove the black king off the board, or compel him to take the piece or pieces thus placed in his power, at his, the adversary's, pleasure.

To show the difference between the moves of a man and a king more clearly, suppose, instead of a king, black had only a man on 29; in that case, the man might go to 22, taking 25, and from 22 to 15, taking 18; but here his exploits would end, as he could not move backward from 15 to take 19, but, on the contrary, he must rest on 15; and, at the next move, would himself be taken, by the white king, on 19, jumping over his head into 10.

When, as we have already explained, all the men, on one side, are taken, or so hemmed in by the opposite colour that they cannot move, the person who has played them is beaten. If, towards the end of the game, one, two, or three kings of each colour be left on the board, and neither player can prevail on the other to risk a move, or if one who is weaker than, or has not the move of the other, be determined to move to and fro in safe squares, where he can never be taken, the game is then drawn, and given up, neither party winning. We shall presently see how two kings may conquer one, or a player with the smaller numerical force can beat his opponent.

THE LAWS OF THE GAME.

I. The board must be so placed that each player has a white double corner at his right hand at his own end of the board.

II. The choice of colour and the first move of the game must be determined by lot, after which each player takes the move alternately.

III. Black moves first, and the players change men with each game.

IV. Pointing over the board, or any other action by which the player prevents his adversary from fully seeing the men, is not allowed.

V. The player who touches a man, except for the purpose of adjusting it on its square, must move it. *A man moved over the angle of a square, must be moved to that square and no other.*

VI. Any piece *en prise* must be taken; and if it be not taken, the player's opponent may "huff" him by removing from the board the man which should have made the capture, and then playing a man of his own. It is optional with a player either to insist on his opponent taking an offered man, or to allow him to "stand his huff."

VII. Five minutes is the maximum time allowed for a move; any player exceeding that time before he moves, loses the game.

VIII. The player who quits the game, or leaves the room during its progress without the consent of his opponent, loses it.

IX. When two kings on one side remain opposed to one on the other, the former player may be called upon by his opponent to win the game in twenty moves, or resign it as a draw, the moves to be counted, twenty on each side, from the time of notice.

X. When there remain three kings opposed to two, the player with the weaker force may call upon his opponent to win in forty moves. If he fail, the game is drawn.

XI. With two kings on each side the game is drawn if one or other player fail to win in forty moves, after receiving notice that his moves will be counted.

XII. A player making a false move must either replace the pieces and make a legal move, or resign the game, at the option of his opponent.

XIII. When several pieces are taken at one move, they must none of them be removed from the board till the taking piece has arrived at its final square; and if the player fail to take all the men he can by the move, his opponent may huff him.

XIV. When a man arrives at the last row of squares on his opponent's side he must be immediately crowned; but he cannot move again till his opponent has moved.

XV. All disputes are to be decided by the majority of the company present.

GAMES FOR PRACTICE.

Remembering the plan of notation shown on the numbered diagram, we may now play a few games in order to familiarize the student with the principles of Draughts. The men may occupy either end of the board; but, for the sake of convenience, we make the black men move first in the following games. A star placed against the figure shows when a man has been taken, and a x where it is made a king. Of course many variations in the moves might be given, but they are not necessary to be shown, since our object is merely to set the student on the right road, leaving him then to attain proficiency by practice.

GAME I.—BLACK TO PLAY AND WHITE TO WIN.

BLACK.	WHITE.	BLACK.	WHITE.	BLACK.	WHITE.
11 to 15	22 to 18	1 to 5	18 to 9*	25 to 22	17 to 13
15 — 22*	25 — 18*	5 — 14*	19 — 15	18 — 23	8 — 4
8 — 11	29 — 25	11 — 18*	20 — 11*	10 — 14	24 — 20
4 — 8	25 — 22	18 — 22	26 — 17*	22 — 18	4 — 8
12 — 16	24 — 20	13 — 22*	11 — 8	18 — 22	20 — 16
10 — 14	27 — 24	22 — 25	8 — 4 к	7 — 10	8 — 11
8 — 12	24 — 19	25 — 29 к	4 — 8	14 — 17	28 — 24
7 — 10	32 — 27	2 — 7	23 — 19	10 — 14	24 — 20
9 — 13	18 — 9*	29 — 25	27 — 24	17 — 21	11 — 8
5 — 14*	22 — 18	14 — 18	21 — 17	14 — 17	8 — 11
					wins.

If Black, at his seventeenth move, had played from 12 to 16 instead of making his king, he would have stood a better chance ; and, instead of moving from 14 to 18, at his twentieth move, he should have played from 25 to 22 and pinned the king.

GAME II.—BLACK TO PLAY AND DRAW THE GAME.

BLACK.	WHITE.	BLACK.	WHITE.	BLACK.	WHITE.
9 to 13	22 to 18	4 to 8	23 to 18	15 to 19	18 to 14
10 — 15	25 — 22	8 — 11	28 — 24	10 — 17*	21 — 14*
6 — 10	18 — 14	12 — 16	24 — 20	2 — 7	22 — 18
10 — 17*	21 — 14*	16 — 19	27 — 23	7 — 10	14 — 7*
15 — 19 (A)	24 — 15*	19 — 24	14 — 9	3 — 10*	18 — 15
11 — 25*	30 — 21*	5 — 14*	18 — 9*	11 — 18*	26 — 23
8 — 11	29 — 25	24 — 28	9 — 5	18 — 27*	31 — 6*
11 — 15	25 — 22	7 — 10	23 — 18	1 — 10*	drawn.

If the variation (A) be made at Black's fifth move, he wins.

VARIATION A.

Moves 1 to 4 on both sides as before.

BLACK.	WHITE.	BLACK.	WHITE.	BLACK.	WHITE.
15 to 18	22 to 15*	17 to 21	25 to 22	30 to 26	24 to 19
11 — 18*	29 — 25	6 — 9 (B)	22 — 18	26 — 17*	19 — 12*
8 — 11	24 — 19	13 — 17	26 — 22	17 — 22	10 — 6
4 — 8	28 — 24	17 — 26*	31 — 22*	22 — 15*	6 — 2 к
1 — 6	24 — 20	9 — 13	19 — 15	15 — 10	20 — 16
6 — 10	32 — 28	12 — 16	30 — 26	11 — 20*	2 — 4*
10 — 17*	23 — 14*	21 — 25	26 — 23		and Black wins.
2 — 6	27 — 24	25 — 30 к	15 — 10		

But if Black play from square 6 to square 10 at his fourteenth move (variation B) he will lose :—

VARIATION B.

BLACK.	WHITE.	BLACK.	WHITE.	BLACK.	WHITE.
6 to 10	22 to 17	8 to 11	26 to 22	15 to 22*	24 to 6*
13 — 22*	26 — 17*	3 — 8	19 — 16		White wins.
11 — 15	31 — 26	12 — 19*	22 — 18		

GAME III.—BLACK TO MOVE AND WHITE TO WIN.

BLACK.	WHITE.	BLACK.	WHITE.	BLACK.	WHITE.
11 to 15	23 to 19	15 to 24*	28 to 19*	16 to 19	7 to 2 K
9 — 14	22 — 17	11 — 16	31 — 26	1 — 6	2 — 9*
6 — 9	17 — 13	16 — 20	26 — 22	5 — 14*	17 — 10*
2 — 6	25 — 22	20 — 24	22 — 17	15 — 6*	29 — 25
8 — 11	22 — 17	24 — 27	17 — 10*	19 — 23	25 — 22
14 — 18	26 — 23	27 — 31 K	30 — 25	23 — 26	22 — 18
4 — 8	23 — 14*	8 — 11	23 — 18	26 — 30 K	18 — 15
9 — 18*	27 — 23	31 — 27	10 — 7	30 — 26	15 — 11
18 — 27*	32 — 23*	3 — 10*	21 — 17	26 — 22	11 — 7
10 — 14	17 — 10	27 — 24	18 — 14	6 — 10	7 — 2 K
7 — 14*	19 — 10*	24 — 15*	14 — 7*	10 — 14	2 — 6
6 — 15*	24 — 19	11 — 16	25 — 21	14 — 9	6 — 10
					wins.

GAME IV.—BLACK TO MOVE AND DRAW.

BLACK.	WHITE.	BLACK.	WHITE.	BLACK.	WHITE.
11 to 15	22 to 17	12 to 19*	23 to 7*	17 to 22	23 to 19
8 — 11	23 — 19	2 — 11*	26 — 23	22 — 26	21 — 17
9 — 13	25 — 22	4 — 8	22 — 18	1 — 6	18 — 14
6 — 9	27 — 23	13 — 22*	18 — 9*	6 — 10	14 — 9
9 — 14	24 — 20	5 — 14*	30 — 25	8 — 12	9 — 6
15 — 24*	28 — 19*	22 — 26	31 — 22*	11 — 15	6 — 2 K
11 — 15	32 — 28	3 — 7	22 — 18	15 — 24*	2 — 11
15 — 24*	28 — 19*	14 — 17	21 — 14*		drawn.
7 — 11	19 — 16	10 — 17*	25 — 21		

GAME V.—BLACK TO MOVE AND WIN.

BLACK.	WHITE.	BLACK.	WHITE.	BLACK.	WHITE.
22 to 18	11 to 15	28 to 19*	14 to 17	19 to 16	12 to 19*
18 — 11*	8 — 15*	25 — 22	9 — 13	23 — 16*	14 — 18
21 — 17	4 — 8	29 — 25	5 — 9	21 — 14*	10 — 17*
23 — 19	8 — 11	32 — 28	9 — 14	24 — 19	15 — 24*
17 — 13	9 — 14	31 — 27	1 — 5	22 — 8*	17 — 21
27 — 23	6 — 9	25 — 21	11 — 15	28 — 19*	21 — 30*K
13 — 6*	2 — 9*	27 — 24	7 — 11	16 — 12	30 — 16*
24 — 20	15 — 24*	30 — 25	3 — 7	20 —	2*K and wins.

GAME VI.—BLACK TO MOVE AND DRAW.

BLACK.	WHITE.	BLACK.	WHITE.	BLACK.	WHITE.
22 to 18	9 to 13	26 to 23	6 to 9	32 to 28	4 to 8
25 — 22	5 — 9	30 — 26	11 — 16	28 — 24	16 — 20
29 — 25	10 — 15	24 — 20	15 — 24*	24 — 19	8 — 11
21 — 17	7 — 10	28 — 19*	3 — 7	19 — 16	20 — 24
25 — 21	1 — 5	20 — 11*	8 — 24*	16 — 7*	2 — 11*
23 — 19	9 — 14	27 — 20*	12 — 16	22 — 18	13 — 22*
18 — 9*	5 — 14*	20 — 11*	7 — 16*		drawn.

HAVING THE MOVE.

We must now draw attention to the importance of *having the move* upon an anta-gonist. The value of this will, no doubt, have frequently occurred to the player in the course of the preceding games; but there are situations when it is not only useless, but detrimental. To have the move when your men are in a proper position, upon an open board, will often, in a short time, give you the power of forcing your adversary into such a situation as will render his defeat certain; but having the move when your men are huddled in confusion together, and you are unprepared to attack from any quarter—that is to say, when you are strong in number, but powerless in position—will, not unfrequently, cause you to lose the game.

In order to know whether any one of your men have the move over one of your adversary's, you must carefully notice their respective positions, and, if your opponent have a black square on your right angle under his man, you have the move upon him. This is a general rule, and will apply to any number of pieces. To illustrate it with an instance:—If white have a man on 22, it being his turn to play, and black's man be on 11, white has the move. There is, however, another and somewhat simpler method of ascertaining whether the player, whose turn it is to play, has the move; namely, by counting the squares and the men; and if the squares be odd, and the men even, or the men odd, and the squares even, then the party whose turn it is to play has the move: thus, if there be a black man on 19, on 26 a white king, on 28 a black king, and on 32 a white man, and white have to play, he has the move, and may certainly win the game; the opposite player's men being even, and the white squares between them and his own odd; there are three white squares from the black king on 28 to the white king on 26 (viz., 24, 27, and 31), and between the black man on 19 and the white man on 32 two white squares, 23 and 27, making together, five. White begins by moving his man to 27, the black king goes to 32, the white man proceeds to 24, and is taken by the black man on 19; the white king now goes to 23; the black king must next step to 27, having no other move (his man being on 28), and is taken by the white king, who thus gets into 32, and wins the game, as black cannot move his man.

ENDINGS OF GAMES.

Two Kings to One.—The player who has two kings to one, towards the end of the game, can always win in at most seventeen moves, by bringing up his men and forcing his opponent's king into the double corner. Suppose your adversary to have retreated to square 32, and you to have brought up your men to squares 23 and 19. If it is his turn to move, he can only move to 28, when you move from 23 to 27; and when he moves back to 32, you from 19 to 23. You can then win in eight moves, at most:—

BLACK.	WHITE.	BLACK.	WHITE.
23 to 27	28 to 32	23 to 18	20 to 16
19 — 23	32 — 28	18 — 15	16 — 12 (or 20)
27 — 32	28 — 24	15 — 11	white must move and
32 — 28	24 — 20		black wins.

A like series of moves will accomplish the same end in the opposite double corner.

Three Kings to Two.—With three kings to two you must give man for man; when, having two to one, you proceed as before. There are several ways of forcing the exchange. You may either drive the weaker force into the side square or get all the men in a line on one of the long diagonals, and then give one for one.

Two Kings to Two.—Two kings to two is a drawn game so long as the players keep the double corners; but if you can get your kings into this or a like position on either side of the board—*Black*, kings on squares 2 and 7; *White*, kings on squares 14 and 15—the kings on the side squares must win. Suppose black has to play: he moves from 7 to 10, when white must take; and whichever way he takes, he loses his two kings.

ADVICE TO YOUNG PLAYERS.

When you sit down to play, make up your mind to win, and consider every move before making it. Look well over the board, and see that none of your men are *en prise*, nor a trap artfully laid for you to fall into. Study not only your own position, but that of your adversary. Never touch a man without moving it; determine your move before you put down your hand, and then make it. When you have the move,

BLACK.

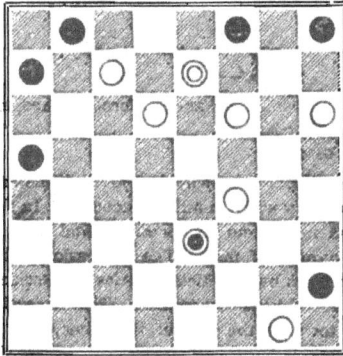

WHITE.

WHITE TO MOVE AND WIN.

pursue your game with judgment and care. Keep your men well towards the centre of the board in a pyramidal shape, taking care to back them up so as to leave no blank squares behind your advanced men. Many players consider that they do well to keep men on their last squares as long as they can. This plan has its advantages, for it prevents your opponent from making kings; but it is also apt to cramp your game. The best plan in commencing the game is to make a few judicious exchanges, so as to open the way for your back men. This you should do by avoiding the side squares as much as possible, and pinning your opponent's men as they advance. Endeavour to march on for a king as soon as you can, as the power possessed by his majesty of moving and taking either backwards or forwards gives him an immense advantage. The above diagram, for instance, exhibits a position in which the king is very powerful. In this case white's initial move is from 12 to 8, when black must take from 3 to 12, and then the game proceeds thus—

WHITE.	BLACK.	WHITE.	BLACK.	WHITE.	BLACK.
6 to 2	23 to 16	5 to 9	17 to 22	4 to 8	16 to 19
10 — 6	1 — 10	9 — 14	22 — 26	8 — 11	19 — 23
7 — 14	16 — 7	14 — 18	26 — 31	22 — 25	31 — 26
2 — 11	5 — 9	18 — 22	4 — 8	25 — 30	
14 — 5	13 — 17	11 — 4	12 — 16		

A false move in this game would have proved fatal to white; therefore, great watchfulness is necessary to success. Numerous like examples might be given, but this will be sufficient to show what we mean. Play with courtesy, and above all, keep your temper.

In the following positions it may seem that the strongest force ought to win, but this is not always the case.

1. *Black.*—Men on squares 32, 31, 27, 25, 24, 22, 21, 19, 17, and 13. *White.*— Men on 18, 16, 15, 12, 10, 8, 7, 5, 3, 2, and 1.

Now black moves and wins. He goes from 24 to 20 and gains two for one, because white must take from 15 to 24. Black afterwards wins one of the men *en prise*, and presently finishes the game.

2. *Black.*—King on 26 and king on 27. *White.*—King on 25, man on 21. In this position black wins, either with or without the move—

BLACK.	WHITE.		BLACK.	WHITE.
27 to 23	25 to 29		26 to 30	25 to 29
23 — 18	29 — 25		18 — 22	

3. *Black.*—King on 19, king on 18, man on 28. *White.*—King on 32 and king on 27.

WHITE.	BLACK.		WHITE.	BLACK.
27 to 24	18 to 15		20 to 24	19 to 15
24 — 20	15 — 11		24 ∟ 20	

And white, with the move, draws the game though with the smaller force, by keeping the command of square 20.

This is exactly the reverse of the ordinary game, and he who first loses all his men wins. It is by no means so easy as it seems to lose your men advantageously. In this game the best squares are the side ones, and it is by no means an unusual thing to compel a single man or king to take a large number of men. The possession of the move is of great importance in the Losing Game, as by a judicious series of sacrifices you may get your opponent into such a position as obliges him to take. The possession of two men (or kings) to one is advantageous towards the end of the game, as with one move you may then force your opponent to take. A little practice will soon make you familiar with this interesting variety of Draughts.

Polish Draughts is sometimes played on a board of 100 squares, 50 of each colour; but in England it is generally played on the ordinary draught-board. With the enlarged board of 100 squares the game becomes much more intricate. The peculiarities of Polish Draughts are—that the men take both backwards and forwards, a square being passed and repassed as often and as long as there is a man *en prise ;* and that the kings travel over any number of diagonals, taking such men as may lie in their way, either in their forward or backward march. Like the bishop in Chess, the king goes to and fro so long as the way is clear, without reference to distance or to the fact of there being more than one square vacant between him and the man *en prise.*

By frequent exchanges and stratagem, and most of all by the possession of a king, the good player can win under apparently difficult and adverse circumstances, the smaller number of men frequently overcoming the greater. The following is an easy example of Polish Draughts:—

BLACK.	WHITE.	BLACK.	WHITE.	BLACK.	WHITE.
23 to 19	11 to 16	25 to 22	14 to 17	18 to 15	9 to 14
26 — 23	8 — 11	21 — 14*	10 — 26*	27 — 23	17 — 21
24 — 20	3 — 8	18 — 15	11 — 18*	28 — 24	8 — 12
27 — 24	9 — 14	20 — 2*κ	26 — 31κ	2 — 13	13 — 17
31 — 27	6 — 9	23 — 14*	9 — 18*	13 — 22*	21 — 30
22 — 18	9 — 13	19 — 16	12 — 19	32 — 27	30 — 10*
18 — 9*	5 — 14*	24 — 22*	31 — 17	27 — 23	10 — ˜7
25 — 22	2 — 6	30 — 25	17 — 21	22 — 8	7 — 11*
22 — 18	6 — 9	25 — 22	21 — 17	23 — 19	14 — 17
29 — 25	1 — 5	22 — 18	5 — 9	20 — 16	11 — 20

And white wins.

CONCLUDING REMARKS.

Those who know little of Draughts are apt to consider it a poor and trifling game; but that it is not so thought by all, the following extract from Dr. Johnson's Dedication to "Payne's Treatise" sufficiently proves:—"Triflers may think or make anything a trifle; but since it is the great characteristic of a wise man to see events in their causes, to obviate consequences, and ascertain contingencies, your lordship will think nothing a trifle by which the mind is inured to caution, foresight, and circumspection."

In conclusion, we beg to assure our readers, that simple as it may appear, they will never be able to attain any proficiency in Draughts without some study, and much caution; for although it does not require one-tenth of the attention necessary to the acquirement of Chess, yet it is totally impossible for our young friends to derive much amusement from the game, if they move the pieces as carelessly as a couple of

Kittens at Play.

BACKGAMMON.

ACKGAMMON is the modern name for the ancient game of "Tables." The word is said to be derived from the Welsh, and to signify a "little battle"; but Strutt says, with some appearance of correctness, that it comes from the Saxon *bac* and *gamen*, a back game: so called because the player brings back his men from his antagonist's tables into his own; or because the pieces are sometimes taken up and obliged to go back, that is, re-enter at the table from which they came. Whatever be the etymology of its name, the game has been long and deservedly a favourite amusement.

Backgammon is a game of chance, in which skill and memory are required. It is played on a marked board with draughtmen, dice and dice-box. The moves of the men are determined by throws of the dice, and, as will be presently seen, the game is won by the player who succeeds in bringing all his men into his own side of the table, and then *bearing* them off the table (as explained hereafter).

The Backgammon-board consists of two parts or tables, generally united by a hinge in the middle, so that they can be shut up like a box. Each table possesses twelve points, six at each end. These points are coloured black and white (or any other contrasted colours) alternately; but the colours have no reference to the game, and are only used to render the counting of the game more easy. The left-hand division on the one side, and the right-hand on the other, is the "home," or inner table, of each player; and according as two or more points appear on the dice thrown from the box, so the men are moved onward from point to point, till all the men of one colour arrive in their separate homes. The insides of folding draught-boards are generally arranged for backgammon.

MODE OF PLAYING THE GAME.

The game is played by two players, who have each fifteen men (usually draught-men), one set being black and the other white. In beginning the game the men are placed on the board in the manner shown in the following diagram, two men on the ace-point on each side, five on the six-point, three on the eight, and five on the twelve. The two dice are common to both players, but each one has his own dice-box, and the throws are taken alternately. The dice are perfect cubes, marked with dots from one to six. French terms are commonly used; thus, one is called *ace;* two, *deuce;* three, *tré* (or *trois*); four, *quatre;* five, *cinque;* and six, *size.* At every throw the two dice are employed; consequently, the player may throw from two (double-ace) to twelve (double-six). If the player throw *doublets,* or two dice of one number, he counts double the number of dots on each dice; thus, by a throw of double-two, he does not count four, but eight.

Suppose the table as arranged in the diagram to be placed between the players, whom we will call black and white. The men move towards their ace-points, and are governed in their moves by the throws of the dice. Thus, white counts round from the ace-point of black, and black counts round from the ace-point of white. These points are seen to have severally two men on them, on opposite corners of the table.

BLACK'S INNER TABLE.   BLACK'S OUTER TABLE.

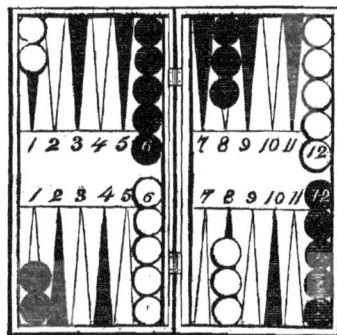

The grand object of the game is for each player to get all his men played round into his inner table, removing them from point to point agreeably to the throws of the dice, and finally *bearing them,* or moving them off the board. The player who first clears his men off the board wins the game.

In throwing, the number upon each die may be reckoned by itself, or collectively with the number on the other die. Thus, if *quatre* be thrown by one die, and *size* by the other, one man can be advanced four points, and another six points; or a single man can be advanced ten points—always providing a point

WHITE'S INNER TABLE.   WHITE'S OUTER TABLE.

is open to allow this movement to it. If doublets are thrown, four men may be moved as many places as there are dots on the dice, instead of one or two, as may be done in the case of ordinary throws. Thus, suppose you throw two deuces, you may move one man eight places, two men four places, or four men two places, always presuming that the road be clear. No man can be moved to a point covered by two of your opponent's men. If such point be covered by only one man—which is called a *blot*—then that man can be hit and be removed from the point, and placed on the bar between the tables, and his place taken by the man who has won it. The removal of a man to the bar throws the player to whom it belongs considerably behind in the game, because the man must remain out of the play till he is *entered* by a throw of the dice turning up the number corresponding to one open point on the adversary's table; after which he is brought round in the same way as are the others in the set to which he belongs. The frequent occurrence of this *taking of a blot* gives an adversary a great advantage, and allows him to win his *gammon*. If, at any time during the game, every point to which you might move is covered by the adversary's men, your men must remain *in statu quo*, and the adversary takes his turn; or if only one man can be played you must play it.

We must explain that there are three kinds of victory—one the winning the *hit*, the second the winning the *gammon*, and the third winning a *backgammon*. The player who has played all the men round into his own table, and by fortunate throws of the dice has borne or played the men off all the points, wins the *hit*. The *gammon* may be thus explained:—When you have got all your men round to your own table, covering every point, and your adversary has a man out, then you are enabled to *bear* or lift your men away. This you do by throwing the dice and removing men from the points corresponding to the spots on the dice. If you can bear all your men away before your adversary has borne off one man, you win the *gammon*, which is equivalent to two games or hits. But if your adversary is able to bear one of his men, before you have borne all yours, then your victory is reduced to a *hit*. If the winner has borne all his men off before the loser has carried all his men to his own table, it is a *backgammon*, and held equal to three hits or games. To win two games out of three is called winning "the *rub*," as at whist.

EXPLANATION OF TECHNICAL TERMS.

Backward Game, one in which the player has not succeeded in moving his men so far onward as his opponent has.

Bar, the division between the inner and outer tables.

Bearing your men is the removing them from your inner table, when you have brought them all round.

Blot, a single man left on any point.

Carrying your men, is the removing them from point to point by throws of the dice.

Covering your man is a move by which you are enabled to place another man in front of a single man, and so prevent your adversary from "hitting a blot."

Doublets, two dice of equal value, as two aces, two threes, etc. Double fives or sixes are called *high doublets*.

Entering your man, is the replacing of your man after he has been hit. No man can be carried forward while another remains to be entered; but meanwhile, the other player goes on with his game.

Forward Game, one in which the player's men are advantageously moved onward by means of high throws, doublets, etc.

Hitting a blot, throwing any number on either of the dice corresponding to the point on which the blot (or single man of your adversary's) is left. The man so hit is taken up and placed on the bar till he can be entered.

Making points, is a term used when a player is rapidly running away from, or gaining on, his adversary.

Points, the several divisions of the tables, as ace-point, the first in the inner table; six, or bar-point, the one next the bar, etc.

The terms, *Men, Table, Gammon,* etc., are sufficiently explained in the text.

LAWS OF BACKGAMMON.

I. If you take a man or men from any point, that man or men must be played.

II. You are not understood to have played any man till you have placed it upon a point and quitted it.

III. If you play with fourteen men only, there is no penalty attending it, because, with a less than the full number, you play to a disadvantage.

IV. If one of two numbers thrown enable a man to enter, the first man must be entered and the second played up to a vacant point; but if more than one man has to enter, and only one number giving the privilege appear on the dice, the latter man must remain on the bar till he can enter.

V. If you bear any number of men before you have entered a man taken up, and which, consequently, you were obliged to enter, such men, so borne, must be entered again in your adversary's tables, as well as the man taken up.

VI. If you have mistaken your throw, and played it, and your adversary have thrown, it is not in your power or his choice to alter it, unless both parties agree.

CONCLUDING REMARKS.

Backgammon is a delightful pastime when indulged in for amusement only; but if once the gambling element is allowed to enter, the board should be put aside, and the dice thrown into the fire; for, even though the stakes may be very small at starting, the temptation to increase them grows imperceptibly, till at last a young man will think no more of risking sovereigns than a boy does of playing at

Catchpenny.

DOMINOES.

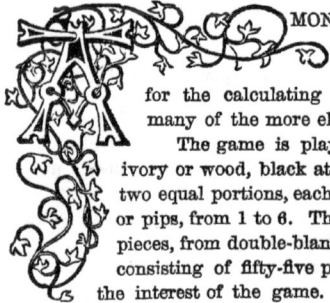

MONG semi-scientific games Dominoes deservedly holds a high place; for, though by many looked upon as rather trivial, it affords capital exercise for the calculating powers, and certainly as much amusement as many of the more elaborate games.

The game is played on an ordinary table, with oblong pieces of ivory or wood, black at the back, the faces being white, and divided into two equal portions, each portion either blank or marked with black spots, or pips, from 1 to 6. The regular set of dominoes consists of twenty-eight pieces, from double-blank to double-six. Sets that go up to double-nine, consisting of fifty-five pieces, are occasionally used, and greatly increase the interest of the game. There are various games with dominoes, the most popular of which we will now proceed to describe. Most of them may be played by two or more players, either singly or in *sides*.

THE ORDINARY GAME.

The dominoes (sometimes called "cards" and sometimes "stones") are shuffled face downwards on the table, and the players each draw one to determine which shall first play. The dominoes are then re-shuffled, and each player takes a certain number, the set being divided equally amongst the players, from the stock on the table, and places them edgeway on the table, or takes them in his hand, so that their pips are

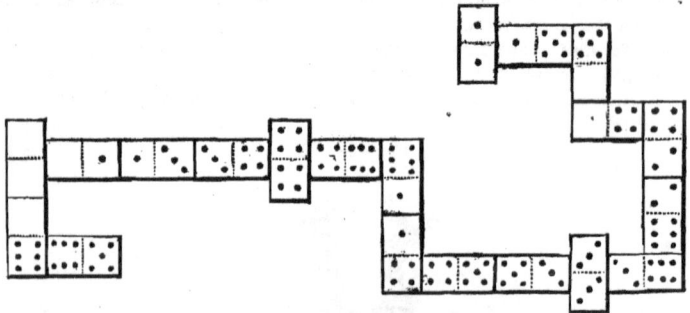

not seen by the other players. He who has drawn the highest domino at the first draw has the *pose*, or privilege of playing first, and then the game proceeds as follows :—

The first player, after arranging his cards, lays one, face upwards, on the table. The next player then plays a domino which has at one end a corresponding number of pips to that at one end of the domino first played, placing it so that the corresponding numbers fall in a line, and then the next, and so on, each domino played corresponding at one of its ends with the number at one end of the line of dominoes already played. In case of a "double," the domino is placed across the line, so that when several pieces have been played, they present some such a figure as that shown in the diagram on the preceding page.

For instance, suppose the first play a double-six, the next may play six-three, and the third double-three, and the fourth a three-one; then, when it comes round to the first player's turn he may put down, say, a double-one, the second a one-four, and the third, who has no corresponding domino, cries " Go !" when the next perhaps plays a double-four, and so on till one of two things occur—either one of the players gets rid of all his dominoes, and so wins the game, or the game becomes *blocked ;* that is, neither player has a domino to match or pair with the number of spots at either end of the row of played pieces. In this latter case, he who has the smallest number of pips left on the dominoes in his hand wins the game. But when a block or "go" occurs with one player, the next goes on if he has a domino that will pair; and if he has not, then the next plays, and if he fail the next, and so on till the game is over.

ALL FIVES.

Two or more players take each a certain number of dominoes, and the object of the game is to make the end pieces count five or multiples of five. Thus, with a double-six at one end and a double-four at the other, the player with the last would count twenty. Say the dominoes are played thus :—The first player plays a double-one, the next a one-three—double-one and three count five, so the second player scores one point; the third a double-three, the fourth a three-six; then the first player puts down a double-six, and the second a one-four at the other end, and the third a double-four: double-four equals eight; double-six, twelve, being together twenty, or four times five, for which the last player scores four points.

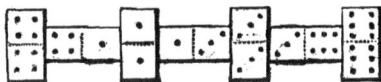

THE MATADORE GAME.

This is a variation of All Fives, and is usually played with a set of dominoes up to double-nine, each player taking five or seven dominoes. The object is to get seven or multiples of seven at the ends when added together, one point being counted for each seven. Thus, the player who starts with seven-seven (= 14) takes two points, and if you succeed in getting a double-nine at one end, and a double-five at the other, you score four points for the twenty-eight. Those dominoes which make seven in themselves, viz., four-three, six-one, five-two, are termed "matadores," and can be played at any stage of the hand, turning either end outwards at your pleasure for your opponent to play at. The double-blank is also a matadore, and can be played at any time. Each player takes the *pose* in turn, and he who first gets the allotted number of points—say, fifteen, twenty, or thirty—wins.

38

THE DRAWING GAME.

In this game each player takes three dominoes, and the one with the *pose* puts down a domino. The other plays a corresponding card if he can; but if he has not such a one in his hand, he draws from the stock on the table till he obtain one that will "go" at either end of the line. Both players draw from the stock as they require a card, but three dominoes must always remain undrawn. He who first succeeds in getting rid of all his dominoes, or has the fewest pips in his "hand" when the play is stopped, wins. The great secret of this game—and indeed all the domino games—is to close the game to your opponents and keep it open for yourself.

DOMINO POOL

May be played by two, three, or four players, either singly or as partners. A description of the *single game* will sufficiently serve to acquaint the reader with the method invariably adopted in this, the great domino game of French players. First they determine as to the order in which they shall sit round the table, by drawing each a domino as the cards lie face downwards. He who gets the highest has the *pose*, and the rest follow according to the value of the cards they draw, from right to left. The dominoes are then shuffled, and each player takes five or seven, as may be agreed on at starting; the *pose* passing in turn to the left till the game is over, when the players again draw for position and start. Fifty or a hundred points are played for, and one of the players keeps the score. The game then proceeds in the usual way till one either plays out or stops the run of the dominoes. Then the scorer marks to the name of each player the number of dots left on his unplayed dominoes, and he who first makes the number agreed on—50 or 100, as may be—is out of the game. But he can re-enter by "starring"—that is, putting into the pool a sum equal to his original stake—when he is placed on the same footing as the player with the highest number. All the players are allowed to star while three remain, but when only two are left, the privilege of starring ceases; and those two either play out or divide the pool. When four persons play, they need not change places, as partners sit opposite each other.

MINOR GAMES WITH BOARDS AND PIECES.

VARIOUS amusing games played with boards and men have been constructed, from time to time, upon the principle of Chess and Draughts. Some of the most simple of them need no description in these pages, because the rules by which they are governed always accompany the apparatus necessary for playing at them. Others, however, are of a somewhat higher class, and require the exercise of patience and ingenuity for their proper development. These we proceed briefly to elucidate, commencing with the favourite game, or rather *study*, of "Solitaire."

SOLITAIRE,

AS its name imports, is a game for a single player; it is played on a board with thirty-three holes, into which as many marbles, or sometimes glass balls of various colours and devices, are placed. The game is commenced by the player removing a marble from any given hole, generally the middle one, and then by passing in a straight line over any other marble into a vacant hole, taking the man that is passed over, as in Draughts. The object of the game is to clear the board of all but one marble, which should be left in the hole from which the first was removed. Now this is by no means so easy as it may appear; and you will find that unless you proceed upon a principle you will not be able to accomplish it. The general principle to be observed is to clear away the side marbles, and work up towards the hole from which you started, and in which you must end the game. There are various ways of performing the task; but in each case you can only jump over one man to a vacant hole beyond, not over two, unless each has a vacant hole beyond it, as in Draughts. In the annexed examples

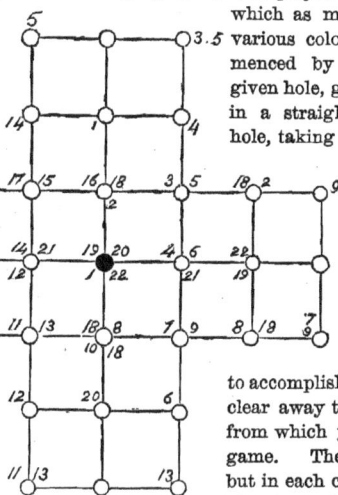

the figures mark the order of march—1 to 1, 2 to 2, etc. In the first Diagram the marble

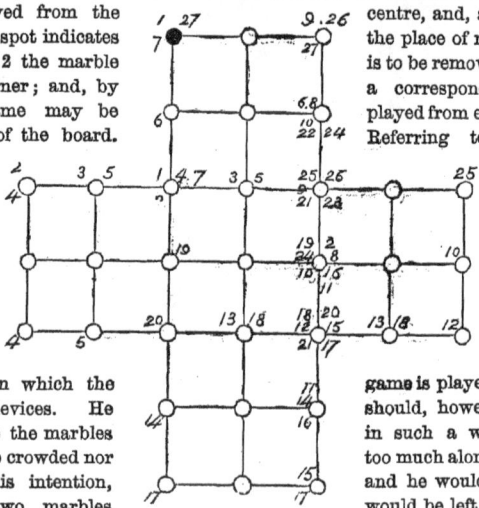

is to be removed from the also, the black spot indicates

In Diagram 2 the marble hand upper corner; and, by moves, the game may be seven corners of the board. again, we find eight places by taking the corresponding the seven other board. There other plans adopted; but reader is ac- the principle on which the to his own devices. He careful to move the marbles them neither too crowded nor would defeat his intention, that at least two marbles such positions as would not allow of the removal of either of them. *Another way of*

centre, and, as in the others the place of removal. is to be removed from the left- a corresponding series of played from either of the other Referring to Diagram 3, we have also of removal marble from positions in sides of the are numerous that may be now that the quainted with game is played, we leave him should, however, always be in such a way as to leave too much alone, as either plan and he would probably find would be left on the board in

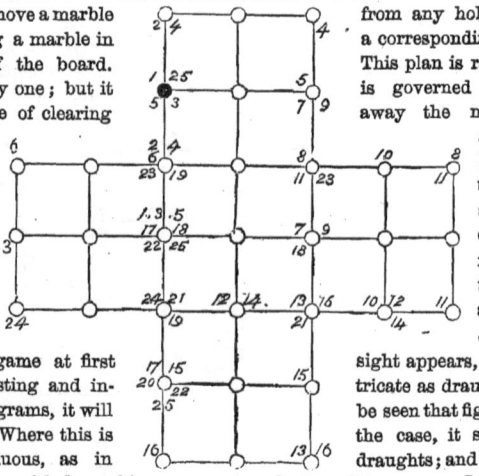

playing, is to remove a marble game by leaving a marble in opposite side of the board. than the ordinary one; but it general principle of clearing distant squares, or three, with ing, to lead up Solitaire may by two persons, ners or oppo- their moves al- with the view of thwarting each simple as the game at first almost as interesting and in- ferring to the diagrams, it will times repeated. Where this is move is continuous, as in

from any hole, and end the a corresponding hole on the This plan is rather more easy is governed by the same away the men from the and leaving two holes interven- to the final move. also be played either as part- nents. They take ternately, either assisting or of other; when, sight appears, it may be made tricate as draughts. [On re- be seen that figures are several the case, it shows that the draughts; and that one marble

is moved into several holes, taking a man at each step of its progress.]

FOX AND GEESE.

This scientific but amusing game may be played either upon a Draught-board or a Solitaire-board, or even upon a sheet of paper marked as in the diagram below, in which the Fox and the Geese are placed in position for beginning the game.

To play Fox and Geese you have seventeen discs of paper or metal, which you call the Geese, and one of a different colour for the Fox, which is placed in the middle, as in the diagram. The object of the game is to confine the Fox in a corner, so that he cannot move out. The Geese march forward on the straight lines, not on the diagonals; and whenever a Goose is on a spot next the Fox, the latter can take him, as in Draughts, by leaping over him, provided there be a va- cant spot be- hind. The Fox can move back- ward, forward, or sideways on the straight lines, but the Geese are not allowed to move back. In order to pin the Fox in a corner, the Geese must go forward one after another in such a way as to fill up all the spots behind, so as to leave the Fox no spot into which he can jump. When the number of Geese is reduced to six it is impossible for them to confine the Fox; but, pro- perly played, the Geese must win. There are other ways of play- ing this game, as by placing the Fox on another spot and altering the arrangement of the Geese. The game may be played so as to make the Fox take all the Geese without being himself taken or confined to any particular square. In the latter case, the Fox chooses his own square at starting. If played on a draught-board, the best position for the Geese—which may be represented by eight white draught-men—is on the two upper rows of squares, 1 to 8; and for the Fox—which may be represented by a king—square 11. If properly moved on the diagonal lines, the Fox must be driven towards the left-hand corner, and pinned in square 29.

AGON, OR THE QUEEN'S GUARDS.

This ingenious and amusing game is, in many respects, akin to Draughts; but the giving piece for piece has no place in Agon, which is won by the attainment of position, and not by the removal of the pieces. Hence, every piece is of equal importance, and the playing at the game begets a habit of regarding the situation of all the men rather than one; showing the advantage of concentrated action. Unless all the pieces are so played as to act simultaneously at the decisive moment for winning the game, all the previous labour is lost; and one piece forgotten, or left too far off, renders it impossible to act effectively.

DIRECTIONS FOR PLAYING.—The game is played on a board divided into hexagonal compartments, and each player has seven pieces, viz., one Queen and six Guards.

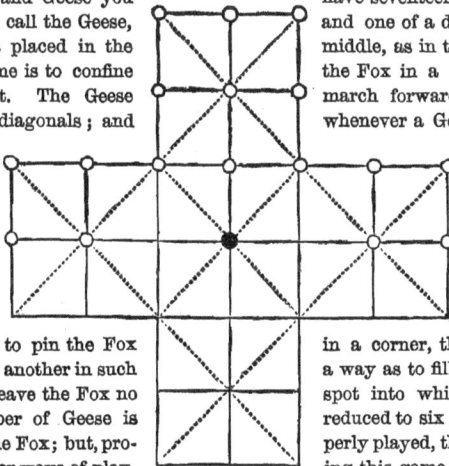

To commence the game the pieces are to be arranged as follows :—Put the two queens on two opposite corners, and the guards on each side of the queens, each colour alternate, with one hexagon left vacant between each piece (two hexagons will be vacant on each side farthest from the queens). See Fig. 1.

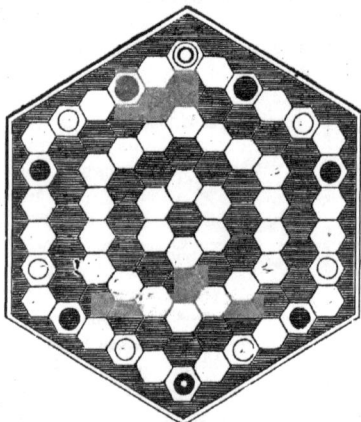

Fig. 1.—Ready to commence the Game.

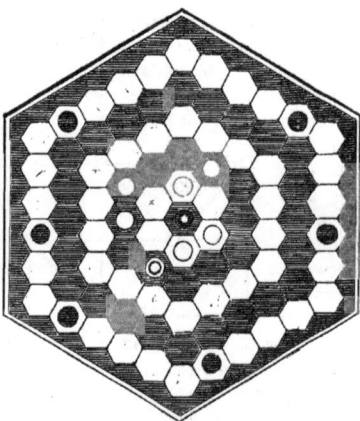

Fig. 2.—The dark Queen, being in a right line between two light pieces, must retire.

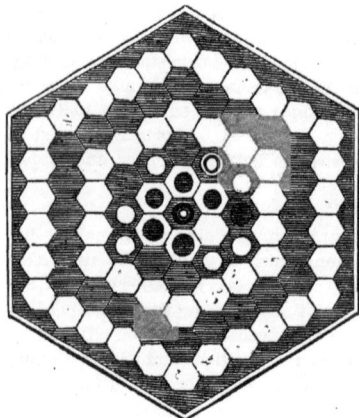

Fig. 3.—The dark piece between two light ones, standing in a right line, must be put back.

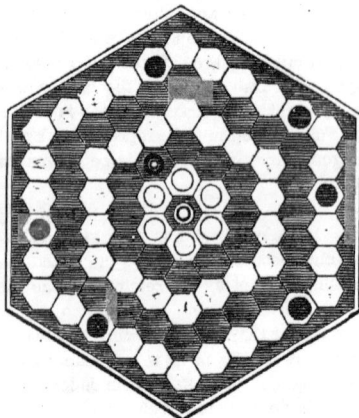

Fig. 4.— The game won by the light pieces.

If the players so agree, the game may be commenced by each alternately placing a piece anywhere on the board, and then, when all the pieces are laid down, each alternately moving forward to obtain the middle.

Having decided which shall move first, the players alternately move a piece towards the centre, one hexagon at a time, or to the next hexagon of the same colour, so that the piece shall remain at the same distance from the centre, it not being allowed to move a piece backward.

Any piece, except the queen, being in a position between two of the adversary's, so that the three pieces form a straight line, must be taken off the board for the next move, and put down anywhere in the outer row. See Fig. 2.

If the queen should be placed in the position between the adversary's, so that the three pieces form a straight line, the queen must be removed for the next move, but may be put in any place, being vacant, the player pleases. See Fig. 3.

That player who can first put all the pieces in the middle, that is, the queen in the centre and the six guards around her, wins the game. See Fig. 4.

Two experienced players may put the pieces in a particular position symmetrically, or otherwise, and, each taking the colours alternately, endeavour to win the game.

LAWS OF THE GAME.—I. None but the queens are to occupy the centre. II. No piece must be moved backwards. III. Of two or more pieces liable to be put back at one time, the queen must be first moved off; any others at the player's option. IV. Any piece touched must be moved, or the move lost. V. Should a player put the six guards in the middle, leaving out the queen, such player loses the game.

HINTS TO PLAYERS.—No advantage will accrue, but, on the contrary, frequently a loss, by throwing back one only of the adversary's pieces, as the piece thrown back may be placed so as to obtain a much better position. As no piece is allowed to move backward, the queens must not be moved into the centre too hastily, as when there (having no move unless thrown out) their usefulness is impaired. The player should endeavour to obtain such a position as to be able to throw back several pieces by following moves, and then move on to the middle before the adversary can overtake or get between the pieces. The surest mode in which to win the game, is to crowd the adversary's pieces as quickly as possible towards the middle, at the same time taking up a position to be able to throw back all his pieces in succession, as soon as an oppor- tunity offers. When a player has the queen in the middle, if not able to win the game, he may often re-open it by bringing a piece against the adversary's, so that if his queen should be thrown back, he may throw back another piece in return ; hence, in throwing back the queens, the greatest caution is always necessary. The player will generally find it advantageous to have one piece at a greater distance from the centre than any of the adversary's ; it must, however, be in a position to get to the middle when the game is drawing to a conclusion. The position shown in Fig. 2 is certain loss of the game to the dark pieces ; the light pieces having forced the dark queen to move into the centre, will be able to throw back a dark piece every move, and thus win the game ; but should the light pieces be moved too early into the middle, it will be impossible to throw back the dark queen without hazarding the reopening of the game.

MERELLES, OR NINE MEN'S MORRIS.

This ancient English game is played with draughtmen, coins, or paper discs, on a table drawn in lines, as in the diagram. Two players have each nine men of different colours. The object of the game is to form rows of three pieces of the same colour, without the intervention of your opponent's men. The first player places a piece on any one of the angles, when his antagonist immediately puts another piece on any angle that may appear likely to prevent the row being formed. As soon as a row be formed, the player who succeeds in making it removes one of his opponent's men, and he who first succeeds in taking all the opposite men but two wins the game. The men may be placed on any of the angles of the lines and be moved backwards, forwards, or diagonally; but as soon as a row is formed, it must remain; but one piece may belong to two or three rows; any of the corner pieces of the squares being capable of forming parts of three rows.

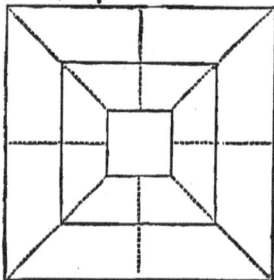

LOTO.

Loto is a sort of arithmetical game for a round party, or it may be played by two boys. The instruments used in the game are a set of twenty-four numbered cards, a quantity of wooden discs, each of which bears a number corresponding to the figures on the cards; about two hundred bone or glass counters, and a bag. Each of the cards contains fifteen numbers, and each number is contained four times in the whole set of twenty-four cards. These numbers are ranged in columns, the units in the first column, the tens in the second, the twenties in the third, the thirties in the fourth, the forties in the fifth, the fifties in the sixth, and so on up to ninety, the highest number. Each card is divided into three rows, and on each row there are nine squares—five of them numbered and four blank, as seen in the diagram. The game commences by choosing a dealer, who shuffles the cards and gives one to each player. If only two or three play, they may have two or three cards each. Having dealt the cards, the leader takes the bag containing the numbered discs, which he draws out rapidly one by one, calling out the numbers as he does so. The player who has a corresponding number on his card to the one called, immediately covers it with one of the glass counters, and he who first succeeds in covering all the numbers on his card wins the game. In order to make Loto interesting, it is usually played for a small pool, made up by an equal

CARD AND DISCS.

contribution from each player, of nuts or other small stake. When so played, he who first succeeds in covering all the numbers in one row takes a fourth of the pool; the player who first covers a second row takes another fourth, and the remainder is given to him who first succeeds in filling all the numbers on his card. The winner of the pool then gathers up the cards, and the game recommences, the players taking it in turns to deal and draw the marked discs from the bag.

The Loto Spelling Game is a different arrangement of the cards, with letters instead of figures; and the object of the play is to spell some word as the discs are drawn out of the bag. It is a very interesting amusement, and provides ample scope for the exercise of memory and dexterity. Loto boxes, with cards, discs, and counters complete, cost from 1s. to 15s. each.

SQUAILS.

This is a new name for the old game of shovel-board, or push-penny. A party of players sit round a table, in the centre of which is a circle marked in divisions. Each player is provided with a coin, or metal or ivory disc, which he pushes with the palm of his hand from the side of the table towards the circle, and the object of the game is to lodge your coin in the centre, and at the same time to force the coins of your opponents away from it.

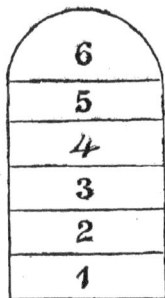

Another plan is to mark the table in divisions, as shown in the margin. Each player has three coins. The first player pushes his coin into division 1; then the second goes on and tries to knock the first player's coin away; and so on till each division has been passed, and one of the players succeeds in lodging his three coins in the last division, 6, and thus wins the game. A good deal of skill is required in avoiding the lines and leaving a coin in the separate divisions.

THE ROYAL GAME OF GOOSE.

In this old-fashioned German game the figure of a Goose is printed on a large sheet of paper, and divided into sixty-three squares or divisions. The object of the players—any number of whom may join in the game—is to make sixty-three points by successive throws of two dice. The first who succeeds in throwing that number wins the pool, which is made up by equal contributions from all the players, who throw alternately, and add the number of each throw to those already made by them. Each player's position on the Goose is marked by a coin, a counter, a pawn, or some small article. Any number beyond 63 sends the thrower back as many points as he exceeds 63. Thus, if he were 58, and he threw 11 by a 6 and a 5, he would go forward 5 squares to 63, and back 6 squares from 63. In addition to this, certain numbers on the Goose are barred, and if the player make them, he is fined two counters, which are added to the pool. A numbered draught-board will serve instead of a Goose.

BAGATELLE.

BAGATELLE stands in the same relative position to Billiards as Draughts does to Chess. Most of our young readers are acquainted with the general form of the Bagatelle-board, and know that the object of the game is to strike the ivory balls with cues into holes made in the bed of the table just as in Billiards the balls are forced into pockets. Much less force in the blow, though not less skill in the player, is necessary for holeing the balls in Bagatelle than are requisite in pocketing and cannoning in the more scientific game. Bagatelle-boards are made of various sizes, from five feet by two to ten feet by three, with slate beds covered with fine green cloth, and surrounded by properly-tempered India-rubber cushions. In the bed of the table are sunk nine cups, or holes, numbered respectively one to nine, and on the side of the board are holes (generally eighty on each side) for scoring the game with pegs. Tables of the best kind, with balls, cues, marking-boards, etc., can be purchased at a cost of from six to twenty guineas. Various kinds of games are played on the Bagatelle-board. The most usual are those known as the English, the French, Sans Egal, and Mississippi.

THE ENGLISH GAME,

Or " La Bagatelle " (as it is often called) *par excellence*, is played by two persons, or any equal number taking sides, with nine balls—usually four red, four white, and one black. The first player places the black ball on the spot in front of the holes, and then placing another ball on the spot at the lower end of the table, strikes it with the cue or mace against the black ball, which must be hit and dislodged before any score can be made. The rest of the balls are then to be played up in the same manner. The object, of course, is to " hole " the balls, and when all the eight balls are played up, which is done one after another by the same player, the numbers of the holes which are filled are counted up and scored to the player, either on the marginal holes with pegs, or on paper or a board. If the black ball is holed it counts double. The first player having played his round, the second player does the same. If more than two players are engaged, one of each side plays alternately. The players, of course, use their best judgment and skill either in striking any of the outstanding balls or cushioning for the holes. There is room for much practice and much exercise of skill in becoming acquainted with the various angles at which the cushions should be struck, and the various degrees of force required, in order to reach certain holes.

Any number of rounds may be played as may be agreed, the player or side which makes the greatest number at the conclusion of the rounds winning the game ; or a score may be played for, usually once up and down the marginal holes with the pegs, viz., 160, the player first getting " out " winning the game, unless he should have played first, when his opponent is entitled to another turn to give him an even chance.

Should there be more than two players engaged, they may at their option all play against each other instead of forming sides.

The position and numbering of the holes are shown in the accompanying diagram. And it will be seen that were all the balls to be holed—which is quite a possible feat for a clever player—the total number that could be scored at one round, supposing black (which counts double) to be in the 9-hole, is 54.

If a ball rebounds from the semicircular head of the table, or from the cushion, and passes back beyond the baulk line (a line at about 18 inches from the player's end of the board, from within which he must play his balls up), such ball is considered dead, and is out of the game for that round. At the commencement of the round, all balls that are played up before the black ball is hit and dislodged from the spot are considered dead, and removed from the board : as is also any ball that is struck off the table. If a ball stops dead on the brink of a hole, it may be challenged by the non-striker, when, if it afterwards rolls in, it does not count, but must be replaced.

THE FRENCH GAME.

This is also played by two persons, or any equal number taking sides. If two

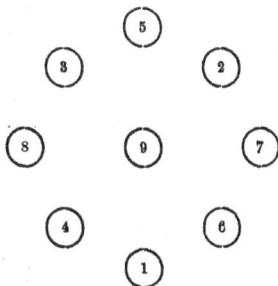

coloured balls are used, one is placed on the spot, and played at with the other, each counting double in the holes in which it falls. The players all take alternate strokes, and the highest aggregate score wins the game. If the coloured ball be missed, the player forfeits five points to his opponent.

SANS EGAL

Is a game played by two persons, who each take four balls of opposite colours. The black ball is placed on the spot in front of the holes. The first player begins by striking one of his balls at the black, the other player following him, and so on alternately. He who holes the black counts it towards his score, as well as all balls of his own colour which he may hole; but on either player holeing one of his adversary's balls the number is scored to the adverse player. The game is usually 21 or 31, as may be arranged between the players.

THE CANNON GAME.

The cannon game consists of cannons alone, or cannons and holes, as may be agreed. If the holes are added to the cannons, the latter count each two points, and the former the numbers marked.

MISSISSIPPI.

In this game the Bagatelle-board is provided with a bridge, marked with numbers over each arch. The object is to play the balls through the arches, and the player reckons the number of each arch which is entered to his score. Two or more balls going through the same arch all count. In order to render the game more difficult, the cushion must be struck with the ball previous to the latter passing through the arch, otherwise the number is scored to the adversary.

COCKAMAROO, OR RUSSIAN BAGATELLE.

This is a game similar to Bagatelle; but the board is provided with a number of little iron pegs or points, with arches, in the centre one of which a bell is suspended, and a channel all round the board. The ball is struck up through this channel, and falls back through the pegs, when certain points are gained according to numbers placed on the board, with additional points if the bell be rung with the stroke of the ball. It is an amusing game for young players, but decidedly inferior to Bagatelle. In Cockamaroo the upper end of the board is elevated in order that the ball may fall back to the player.

CONCLUDING REMARKS.

In playing all these games the ball must be struck with gentle firmness, the cue being held lightly between the fingers and thumb, and not grasped. The side-stroke, and the division of the object-ball (as explained in the section on Billiards), may be properly introduced in order to make the necessary angles. The most scientific strokes are those which are played against the cushion in order to hole a ball in the side-cups, or to drop in a ball that lies in the vicinity of the hole. Hard play at Bagatelle is destructive to success; and if you strike your ball rather low, you have a better chance of holeing it than if you strike too high.

ILLIARDS stands at the head of indoor athletic games, and contains within itself such a combination of skill and chance as to render it a great favourite with players of almost every nation in the world. It was probably known at an early period, as Shakespeare speaks of it in his play of "Antony and Cleopatra." Its origin is generally attributed to the French; but—as in the case of Croquet and other modern games—Billiards is probably an improvement upon some old sport which was common alike to our Saxon ancestors and their Norman conquerors.

THE BOARD AND THE INSTRUMENTS.

Billiards is played upon an oblong board covered with fine green cloth, provided with six netted pockets, one at each corner, and one in the centre of the length of the board on either side. All round the outer edge of the table there is an elastic cushion of India-rubber, also covered with cloth. The bed of the table is of slate, and the table itself stands upon six legs. The regular dimensions of a full-sized billiard-table are twelve feet by six, forming two equal squares inside the cushion. Smaller tables are made for use in private houses. But whatever the size of the table, it is indispensable that it stand perfectly firm and level.

The instruments used in Billiards are ivory balls, varying in size from two inches in diameter, according to the dimensions of the table; and cues, which are smooth, tapering, wooden rods, tipped at their smaller ends with leather. Sometimes ladies play with a mace, which is a hammer-headed cue; but it has nearly gone out of fashion. The height and weight of the cue depend much upon the taste of the player, but one that will stand upright beneath the chin will generally be found the proper length.

PRELIMINARY INSTRUCTIONS.

The object of all the games played on the billiard-table is the forcing the ivory balls into the pockets, by striking one ball against the other with the cue; and the making of caramboles or cannons. Cannons are made by the player striking two balls successively with his own ball.

The first thing the tyro has to learn is to strike the ball properly. This he does by placing his left hand on the table behind the ball to be struck, so as to form a rest or bridge for the cue. A glance at the illustration below will show how the bridge is

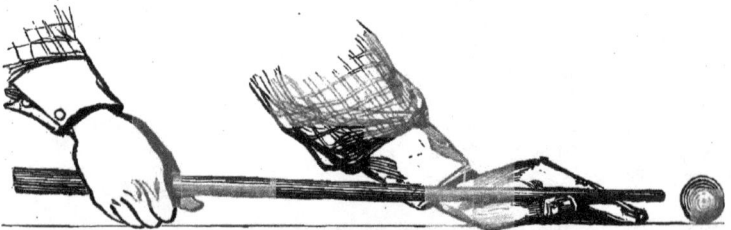

made, and the ball struck. The bridge-hand should be well hollowed, and rest upon the wrist and the tips of the fingers, with the thumb a little extended, so as to give free play to the cue, which rests in the channel between the forefinger and the thumb. The cue is held lightly in the right hand, neither grasped too heavily nor held too daintily. Having pointed his cue towards the ball, the player draws back his right hand, and then, with one free, easy impulse, drives the ball in the direction he wishes it to take, either towards another ball or the cushion, as the case may be. To prevent it from slipping off the face of the ball, the top of the cue is finely roughened with sand-paper and kept chalked. Much of the success of the player depends upon the making of a good bridge, and the holding of the cue nearly parallel to the top of the table, at such a distance from either end as will leave about as much weight in front of the hand as behind it. This is called the "balance of the cue."

GENERAL DESCRIPTION OF THE GAME.

In commencing a game certain uniform methods are adopted. All billiard-tables are provided with a baulk line and baulk semicircle at their lower ends, and three spots—one in the centre of the table, one at the upper end about a foot from the cushion, and one midway between the other two. The latter is called the "pyramid spot," and the one at the end of the table, "the spot." In the ordinary game of Billiards with three balls—two white and one red—the red ball is placed on the spot at starting, and the first player strikes at it with his own ball, or gives a miss. The white balls are severally known as the "plain ball" and the "spot ball," from the latter having a small black spot inserted in order to distinguish it from the other. The second player then strikes his own ball from baulk at either of the balls, if the white be beyond the baulk; and then the game proceeds by each taking alternate strokes at the balls on the table till one or the other succeeds in making a cannon or pocket. The player goes on striking at the balls as long as he can continue to pocket a ball or cannon. If the red ball is forced into a pocket, the player scores three points for what is called a "red winning hazard;" and the red ball is replaced on the spot. If he strike the red, and by the same action play his own ball into a pocket, he scores three for a "red losing hazard," and then makes his next stroke from the baulk. A white ball played into a pocket is either a "winning" or a "losing" hazard, according to whether the object ball or the player's ball fall into the pocket. The "player's ball" is the one struck with his cue; the "object ball" is the one struck with the ball of the player. For every white hazard, two points are scored; and for every cannon also two points; if the player make a cannon and hazard by the same stroke, he scores the points for each; thus he may make four, five, six, seven, eight, nine, or ten points at a single stroke. In the latter case, he must strike the red ball first, make a cannon, and pocket all the balls.

If the player miss a ball, his opponent scores one point, and if he force his ball off the table or into a pocket without striking an object ball, he makes what is called a *coup*, and loses three points. The progress of the game is recorded on a marking-board, which is always sold with the table.

In order that the reader may more fully understand the ordinary way of playing, we extract the following, with permission, from Captain Crawley, one of the acknowledged authorities on the modern methods of billiard-play :—

THE WINNING, LOSING HAZARD, AND CARAMBOLE GAME.

This game is played with three balls, two white and one red. It is made up of winning and losing hazards, cannons, misses, and various penalties for foul strokes. The red ball is placed on the spot at the commencement of the game. The players then string for lead and choice of balls ; and he who loses the lead either begins playing by striking at the red ball, or by giving a miss in baulk. If the first player give a miss, or fail to score off the red ball, the second player goes on and tries to score by making a hazard or cannon. If he succeed, he goes on striking at the balls till he miss a stroke and fail to score. And so the game proceeds, each player making as many as he can off his break till the allotted 50 or 100 points be reached—he who first makes the required number winning the game.

Stringing for the Lead is done in this way : each player places his ball within the baulk semicircle, and strikes it with the point or butt-end of his cue to the top-cushion; and the player of the ball which stops nearest to the cushion at the baulk-end of the table wins the lead, and chooses his ball. It is generally considered a slight disadvantage to lead off, as there is only one ball, the red, to play at. But between equal players, the disadvantage is so little that either of them starts without stringing. Where points are given, the receiver of the points usually leads off; but this is not imperative, as the points are given to equalize the game.

POOL

Is played by two or more players, each of whom has a coloured ball. Each player has three *lives*, or chances, and each takes his turn to play at his opponent's ball, and drive it into a pocket. For every ball so pocketed the owner of the ball loses a life to the player who pocketed it, and for every miss the striker also loses a life. When all but one of the players have lost their lives, the game is won by the player who retains a life or lives; or if two players are left each with an equal number of lives, they may either divide the game or play it out.

PYRAMIDS

Is played with fifteen balls arranged in a pyramid with the apex towards the player. The game, which is generally played for a stake upon the game and a small sum for each ball pocketed, consists entirely of winning hazards. As every billiard-table is accompanied by a set of rules for the several games, it is not necessary to give the laws of Pool and Pyramids.

There are several other games—as the White Winning Game, the Cannon Game, etc.—as well as several foreign games; but as we have shown the general principles of Billiards in the directions and rules, further details are not needed.

TECHNICAL TERMS COMMON TO ALL BILLIARD GAMES.

Angled balls are those which stop in a corner in such a way as not to allow the player to strike them out so as to hit the object ball.

Baulk, the line drawn at the lower end of the table.

Baulk-circle, the semicircle struck from the baulk line. A ball is said to be *in baulk* when it is below the line; and when so placed cannot be played at with a ball in hand.

Break.—A break is a succession of hazards or cannons without an intervening miss.

Breaking the balls is the striking the red from the spot at the beginning of a game.

Bricole, a ball struck against a cushion in order to make a cannon or hazard on its recrossing the table.

Butt, a heavy cue with a broad base, with which the ball may be struck in giving a miss. *Long-butt* and *half-butt*, are long cues for playing at a ball beyond the reach of the player.

Cannon or *Carambole.*—When two balls are struck in consecutive order by the player's ball the double stroke is termed a cannon.

Coup, a stroke in which the player's ball runs into a pocket or goes off the table without striking an object ball.

Doublet, a ball struck against an object ball, so as to make the latter rebound from a cushion towards a pocket.

Full-stroke, half-ball, etc.—The player's ball struck full against the centre of the object ball, is termed a "full stroke;" if the balls come into less contact with each other, the stroke is known as a "half-ball," or a "fine ball;" and when the player's ball strikes the object ball in such a way as to cause both balls to fly off in corresponding, or nearly corresponding angles, such stroke is called *dividing the object ball;* when *side* (explained elsewhere) is put on the player's ball, and it strike the object ball half full, such a stroke is described as *dividing both balls*.

Hazard, a ball pocketed after coming into contact with another ball. When the striker's ball is pocketed after contact with the object ball, it is termed a *losing hazard;* if the object ball be pocketed, the stroke is called a *winning hazard*. A *double hazard* is a stroke which forces two balls into separate pockets, or into the same pocket.

In hand, a ball after being pocketed is said to be in hand, or off the table.

Miss, a ball which, on being struck by the player's cue, fails to touch the object ball. *Giving a miss* is playing a ball out of baulk to a place of safety.

Rest, a cue provided with a hammer-head, or cross of metal or wood, on which to rest the player's cue when his ball is beyond his reach by the ordinary bridge.

LAWS OF BILLIARDS.

I. The game commences by stringing for the lead and choice of the balls. [This rule applies to all English Billiard-games. In stringing for the lead the feet of the player should be behind the baulk, and not at the side of the table. If in stringing the player's ball strike the other, the players string over again.]

II. The red ball must be placed on the spot; and replaced there when it is pocketed, or forced over the edge of the table, or when the balls are broken. ["Breaking the balls" is the replacing them as at the beginning of the game—the red on the spot, and each player's ball in hand—when he who has to break the balls plays at the red, or gives a miss. The balls are said to be broken when the first player has struck the red or given a miss.]

III. A player making a stroke in a game must finish that game, or consent to lose it.

IV. The striker who makes any points continues to play until he ceases to score, by missing a hazard or otherwise.

V. If, when the cue is pointed, the ball should be moved without the striker intending to strike, it must be replaced; and if not replaced before the stroke be played, the adversary may claim it as a foul stroke. [This is to say, a ball moved accidentally must be replaced as nearly as possible. This law is intended to meet cases in which a ball is under a cushion, or angled in a corner. If the player fail to strike *his own ball*, he can make the stroke over again.]

VI. If a ball spring from the table, and strike one of the players, or a bystander, so as to prevent its falling on the floor, it must be considered as off the table. [The penalty is the loss of three points if the player's ball has not first struck a ball on the table; but if a ball has been so struck, no forfeit can be claimed.]

VII. When a ball runs so near the brink of a pocket as to stand there, and afterwards falls in, it must be replaced, and played at, or with, as the case may be. [The challenging a ball, as in Bagatelle, is not allowed in Billiards.]

VIII. A ball lodged on the top of a cushion is considered off the table.

IX. When the player's ball is off the table (in hand), and the other two balls are in baulk, the possessor of the ball in hand cannot play at the balls in baulk, but must strike his ball beyond the semicircle, or play at a cushion out of baulk. [In such a case, the player may use a butt, or play with the butt-end of his cue, and strike at a cushion out of baulk, so that his ball on its return may hit the balls in baulk for a cannon or hazard.]

X. *A line-ball* cannot be played at by the striker whose ball is in hand. [A line-ball is so-called when its centre is exactly on the line of the baulk, in which case it is to be considered in the baulk, and cannot be played at, except from a cushion out of the baulk.]

XI. Every miss purposely made must be given with the point of the cue, and the ball is to be struck only once; if otherwise given, the adversary may claim it as a foul stroke. [But the player may give a miss in baulk with the butt-end of his cue, when he plays his ball to the top-cushion.]

XII. No player can score after a foul stroke. [The following are *foul strokes :*—If the striker move a ball *in the act of striking* and fail to make a stroke; or if he play with the wrong ball; or if he touch his own ball twice in playing; or if he strike a ball while it is running; or if he touch his opponent's ball with hand or cue; or if his feet be off the floor when playing. The penalty in all these cases is losing the lead and breaking the balls. Enforcing the penalty for a foul stroke is entirely at the option of the adversary.]

XIII. If the adversary neglect to enforce the penalty for a foul stroke, the striker plays on, and scores all the points that he made by the foul stroke. [Thus, if a foul stroke be made, and not called, it cannot be enforced after the next stroke is made.]

XIV. *Two* points are scored for every white hazard, *two* for every cannon, and *three* for every red hazard.

XV. When the red ball is pocketed, or off the table, and the spot on which it should stand is occupied by the white ball, the red must be placed in a corresponding situation at the other end of the table; but if that should also be occupied by the other white ball, the red must be placed on the spot in the centre of the table, between the two middle pockets; and wherever it is placed, there it must remain until it be played, or the game be over.

XVI. If a ball be moved by the striker *in taking aim*, such moving of the ball must be considered a stroke. [This appears to be a contradiction of Law V.: but there, it will be remembered, the player did not *intend* to strike the ball moved; here he is in the *act of striking*; and if, while in the act of striking, the ball be moved ever so little, it must be considered a stroke; except, of course, that your opponent may allow you to replace your ball and amend your stroke. This applies equally whether the striker's ball be in hand or not, and whether it go out of baulk or remain in the semicircle.]

XVII. If the player miss striking either ball he loses *one* point; and if by the same stroke his own ball runs into a pocket, he loses *three* points. [That is to say, his opponent scores the points forfeited by the miss or the coup. All misses count towards your adversary's game.]

XVIII. If the striker force his own or either of the other balls over the table, after having struck the object-ball, or after making a hazard or cannon, he neither gains nor loses by the stroke, and his adversary plays on without breaking the balls.

XIX. If the striker *wilfully* force his ball off the table without striking another ball, he loses three points; but if the ball go over by accident, he loses one point only for the miss.

XX. If the striker play with the wrong ball, and a cannon or hazard be made thereby, the adversary may have the balls broken; but if nothing be made by the stroke, the adversary may take his choice of balls the next stroke, and with the ball he chooses he must continue to play until the game is over.

XXI. The playing with the wrong ball must be discovered before the next stroke is played; otherwise no penalty attaches to the mistake, and the player goes on and scores all the hazards he makes.

XXII. No person, except his adversary, has a right to inform the player that he has played, or is about to play, with the wrong ball.

XXIII. If the adversary do not see the striker play with the wrong ball, or, seeing it, do not choose to enforce the penalty, the marker is bound to score all the points that may have been made by the stroke.

XXIV. If the striker's ball be in hand, and the other two balls within the baulk, and he should, either by accident or design, strike either of them, without first playing out of the baulk, his adversary has the option of letting the balls remain as they are, and scoring a miss—of having the ball so struck replaced in its original position, and scoring a miss—of making the striker play the stroke over again—or of counting it as a foul stroke and breaking the balls.

XXV. If the striker's ball be in hand, he must not play at a cushion within the baulk, in order to strike a ball that is out of it. [Should he do so, his opponent can insist on his playing the stroke over again.]

XXVI. When the striker plays at a ball near to his own with the point of the cue, the stroke is fair; but if he play it with the butt-end, the marker must decide whether the stroke be foul or fair. [All strokes are fair with the point of the cue. In pushing-strokes, the point or butt of the cue must only touch the ball once. If the ball be touched and the cue be withdrawn by ever so little, and the ball be again touched, pushed, or struck, such stroke is foul.]

XXVII. When a ball is on the brink of a pocket, if the striker, in drawing back his cue, knock the ball into the pocket, he loses *three* points, as for a coup.

XXVIII. In giving a miss from baulk, should the player fail to strike his ball out of baulk, his adversary may either let it remain so or compel him to play the stroke over again. [The law applies to balls in hand. If the player's ball be already within the baulk line, he can play it, with the point of his cue, to any part of the baulk; and such ball cannot be struck by the other player, if his ball be also in hand, unless he first play at a cushion out of baulk. Intentional misses can be played either in baulk or out of it. The miss may be either played from the end or the side cushion.]

XXIX. When the striker, in giving a miss, makes a foul stroke, his adversary may claim it as such, and enforce the penalty. In such a case, the point for the miss is not scored.

XXX. No person is allowed to take up a ball during the progress of the game without permission of the adversary. [The player who illegally takes up a ball that is in play during the progress of a game, loses the game. In fact, neither player is allowed to touch a ball except it be in hand; that is to say, he may not touch it in order to alter its position. He may, however, lift it to ascertain whether it be the spot ball or the plain ball, when any doubt exists as to its identity.]

XXXI. A ball in play that is moved by accident by either of the players, or by a looker-on, or by the marker, must be replaced, as nearly as possible, to the satisfaction of the player's adversary.

XXXII. The player may have the balls replaced if his adversary accidentally take up a ball that is in play; or he may insist on his adversary breaking the balls.

XXXIII. Neither the player nor his adversary is allowed to obstruct the course of a ball in play, under the penalty of a forfeit for a foul stroke and the breaking of the balls.

XXXIV. If the striker's ball, when it ceases to roll, touch his opponent's ball, no score can be made, and the latter must break the balls. [The striker in this case may run his ball into a pocket, or make a cannon by playing it on to the third ball. If he do either of these, the balls must be taken up, and the red placed on the spot, when the adversary plays from baulk, as at the beginning of the game; that is to say, he "breaks the balls." But if the striker fail to cannon or pocket his own ball, all the balls remain, as they are when they cease rolling, and the other player goes on as usual. It is necessary that the marker or some disinterested person should determine as to the balls touching, for they may be very close together, and yet not actually touch each other. · If the red ball and the adversary's ball touch each other, they may be played at by the striker.]

XXXV. The decision of the marker shall be final on all points of dispute.

ADVICE TO YOUNG PLAYERS.

It is generally considered bad play to pocket your adversary, except when you want to keep the baulk or finish the game. There are, of course, positions in which it would be good policy to pocket the white ball; but as, by so doing, you leave only one (the red) to play at, you reduce your chances by just one half.

If you are uncertain about your side-stroke, do not attempt to give the miss from the side-cushion, but play at the red, and endeavour to bring your own ball into baulk. Place your ball on one of the end-spots of the baulk semicircle, and strike the red by a half-ball; the blow being given to your own ball just above its centre. This will bring your ball back again into baulk, and leave the red under the side-cushion, just above the middle pocket.

Every stroke should be made with a definite object, and if there is no hazard or cannon apparent, play to leave yourself safe. Never strike at the balls at random.

It is often good policy, when you cannot score, to strike gently your opponent's ball, or the red, so as to leave it under the cushion.

Be careful how you vary your style; unless there is obvious reason for a high or a low stroke, a side-stroke or a screw, play an ordinary stroke, and divide the object-ball. Do not experimentalize without a direct purpose.

An advantageous miss when you are under the cushion may save your game.

Remember that it is not only the hazard before you that you have to make, but the hazards that will be left after your stroke. Good judgment in anticipating the consequences of your stroke is therefore a primary element of success. White winning hazards should be played gently, so that, should you fail to make them, your opponent's ball may be left under the cushion. Red winning hazards should, on the contrary, be made with strength enough to bring the ball away from the cushion, if you do not succeed in lodging it in the pocket. Knowledge of strengths is half the battle at Billiards.

VARIOUS STROKES.

In the following diagrams the young player will discover the direction to be taken by the ball after leaving the cue:—

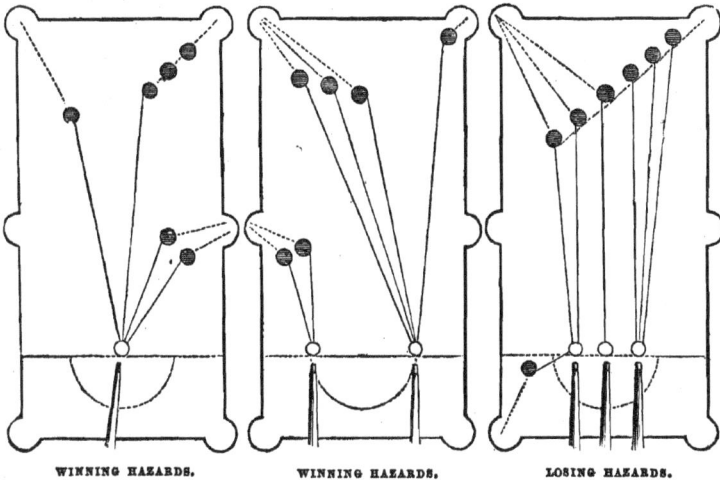

WINNING HAZARDS.   WINNING HAZARDS.   LOSING HAZARDS.

In order to make hazards and cannons with any kind of success, you must remember that the direction taken by your ball after striking the object-ball, will be the counterpart of the direction between the cue and the object-ball; in other words, the angle of reflection is equal to the angle of incidence. When the lines of angle between the two balls and the pocket, or between the three balls necessary to a cannon, do not appear to equal each other, the player makes them do so by dividing the object-ball, or by putting "side" on his own ball.

By this is meant that the amount of force employed in striking the object-ball

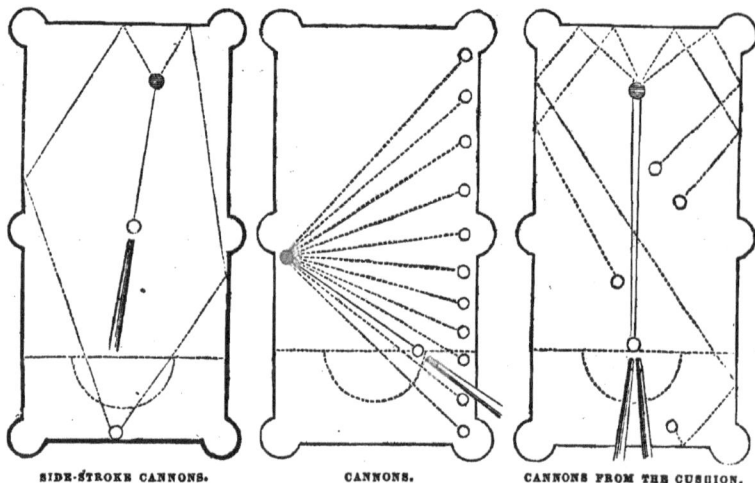

SIDE-STROKE CANNONS.   CANNONS.   CANNONS FROM THE CUSHION.

and the precise point of contact between the player's ball and the object-ball must be regulated according to circumstances. If the object-ball be struck full, the two balls will travel in the same direction; if it be struck smartly in such a way that the side of the one ball meet the side of the other, the direction taken by them after contact will be opposite to each other, and they will depart at angles more or less wide according to the amount of impingement between them. Thus, in making the strokes shown in the diagrams, the amount of contact between the two balls will invariably govern their direction; or, according to this amount of contact will be the deviation of the balls from the line of aim; the smaller the contact, consistent with the strength at which the ball is struck, the wider the angle between the direction of the balls.

Great accuracy of eye and nicety of calculation are necessary in so apportioning the quantity of contact between the player's ball and the object-ball, as to make one or both of them travel in the direction intended, either in making a cannon or pocket. This accuracy of aim in dividing the object-ball can only be acquired by practice.

THE SIDE-STROKE.

There is another method of calculating the proper amount of force necessary, namely, by the "side-stroke." "If," says Captain Crawley, "you strike a ball on its side, it will, while rolling forward, also spin on its axis towards the side on which it is struck. On contact with another ball, or the cushion, the forward roll will be diminished or alto-

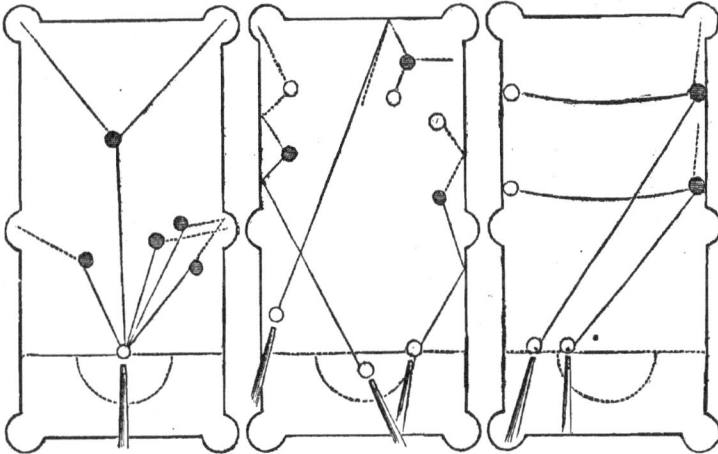

LOSING HAZARDS. SIDE-STROKE CANNONS. SIDE-STROKE CANNONS.

gether stopped, according to the force of the spin, while the axial roll is continued. The result of this is, that the spin causes the ball to roll in the direction of this latter rotation.

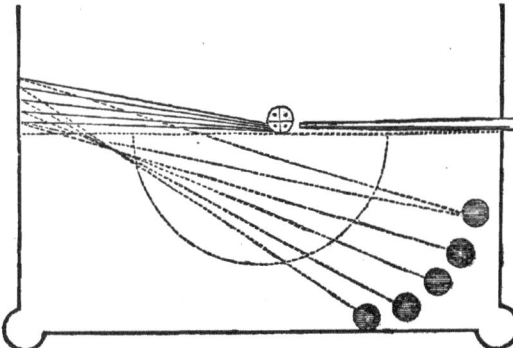

PLAYING A BALL OUT OF BAULK—ILLUSTRATING THE SIDE-STROKE.

It follows from this that you must always strike the ball on the side towards which you wish it to go. The proper effect of the side-stroke is not seen till after contact with the object-ball or cushion; when, if the ball has been struck on its right side, it will travel to the right; if on its left side, to the left. To increase the divergence, you must put on more 'side,' as it is termed, which means that you must hit your ball more towards the outside. In making a side-stroke you must recollect that in hitting your ball very much towards its side, the cue is apt to slip; to prevent which its tip must be well chalked. Most players use a little side-stroke without intending to do so, it being difficult always to strike the ball exactly in its centre."

No better mode of practising the side-stroke can be found than playing your ball against the side cushion from the baulk outside the line, and bringing it back within the line, first on one side and then on the other, by putting on corresponding "side." This is shown in the diagram on the preceding page, in which we see how a ball struck on its side will return into baulk at an angle more or less wide, according to the amount of strength and side employed. With the scientific player the quantity of "side" is a matter of nice calculation, as the progress of a ball struck on its side is rendered slower than usual; but after contact with another ball or the cushion, it flies off at an angle more or less wide, according to the force of the original impetus. To make the side-stroke successfully, the cue must be held a little diagonally to the ball, the player at the same instant giving a very slight twist of the wrist, so as to produce a sort of rubbing motion of his cue's tip on the ball.

THE SCREW.

If you hit the ball high above its horizontal centre, it travels faster than usual; if you hit it below, and at the same time with a sudden drawback of your hand, the ball will go more slowly than when hit full, and either stop at the point of contact with the other ball or return towards the striker. This is called the "screw," a most useful stroke in all game at Billiards, especially at Pool and Pyramids.

CONCLUDING REMARKS.

Though Billiards may be justly considered as the most scientific of the athletic games, the beginner need not be deterred by its apparent difficulties; for no sooner will he commence his practice than they will vanish imperceptibly. To refrain from joining in a game till you thoroughly understand it, is about as wise as determining not to bathe till you know how to swim. First accustom yourself to knock about the balls for amusement, and you will soon acquire enough dexterity and knowledge to enable you to make a stand against many a man who considers himself

A Very Vigorous Player.

www.ingramcontent.com/pod-product-compliance
Lightning Source LLC
Chambersburg PA
CBHW030916150426
42812CB00045B/79